THE TOFFEES

A Concise Post-War History of Everton

DEAN HAYES

The Parrs Wood Press
MANCHESTER

First Published 2000

THE PARRS WOOD PRESS
St Wilfrid's Enterprise Centre
Royce Road, Manchester, M15 5BJ
www.parrswoodpress.com

© Dean Hayes

ISBN: 1 903158 15 X

Cover design by Glenn B. Fleming

Printed in Great Britain by:

MFP Design & Print
Longford Trading Estate
Thomas Street
Stretford
Manchester M32 0JT

CONTENTS

APPENDIX:

ACKNOWLEDGEMENTS

I would like to express my grateful thanks to the following organisations who helped in the compilation of this book: Everton Football Club, the Football League Ltd., the Association of Football Statisticians, Liverpool Central Library and the Harris Library. Many thanks, too, to the Lanacshire Evening Post and the Liverpool Daily Post & Echo for providing most of the photographs in this book. I would also like to express my gratitude to Andy Searle of The Parrs Wood Press for supporting the series of concise post-war histories of north west football clubs.

ABOUT THE AUTHOR

Dean Hayes is an experienced and prolific freelance sports writer specialising in football and cricket. He was educated at Hayward Grammar School, Bolton and West Midlands College of Physical Education and before taking up writing full-time four years ago, he was a primary school headmaster. Having played as a goalkeeper in the Lancashire Amateur League, he now concentrates solely on the summer sport. This former cricket professional, now playing as an amateur, has taken over 2,000 wickets in League Cricket. Dean is married with a son and two step-cildren.

The Toffees

A
CONCISE
POST-WAR HISTORY
OF
EVERTON

Everton, who won the League Championship in 1938-39, were one of the last major English clubs to appoint a manager. Their first such appointment was made in 1939 when they gave the job to club secretary Theo Kelly. Although he was a hard-working and efficient administrator who had outstanding organising ability, Kelly was never particularly popular with the players.

During the Second World War, football was regionalised and players, most of whom were in the services, turned out as 'guests' for teams near their stations.

In April 1944, seventeen Everton players shared a total of £5,500 as accrued benefit, the club's gesture to reward their loyalty in attempting to fulfil playing commitments during the war. In November 1945, Tommy Lawton, whose transfer was also sought by Arsenal, Crystal Palace, Millwall and Nottingham Forest, joined Chelsea for £11,500. At Everton he had scored 70 goals in 95 games but went on to clock up a career total of 231 goals in 390 league games, winning 23 England caps and scoring 22 goals for his country.

Everton's first team on the resumption of the League Championship in 1946-47 was:

G.Burnett; G.Jackson; N.Greenhalgh; J.Mercer; T.G.Jones; T.Watson
J.McIlhatton; E.Wainwright; H.Catterick; W.Fielding and W.Boyes.

So only four regulars from the Championship side began the new campaign as Brentford won 2-0 in the opening match at Goodison Park. Joe Mercer, who had been the bedrock of Everton's pre-war Championship team, returned from his war-time duties to discover that Everton had already appointed a captain in his absence, despite the fact that he was the current England captain. Mercer became very depressed and even contemplated retirement but after 12 games in his old position of left-half, he was transferred to Arsenal in December 1946 for £7,000. In a short space of time, three of the club's best-ever players - Dixie Dean, Tommy Lawton and Joe Mercer - had all departed from Goodison unhappy.

Kelly did not believe in buying players and on the one occasion he did attempt a major signing, that of Newcastle United's Albert Stubbins, he allowed neighbours Liverpool to get the better of him. In his first season at Anfield, Stubbins went on to help the Reds lift the title.

TED SAGAR

Ted Sagar was one of the greatest goalkeepers of all-time. His career as an Everton player spanned 24 years, during which time he played in 495 League and Cup games.

Sagar joined the Toffees from Thorne Colliery in March 1929 after he had had a trial with Hull City and stayed at Goodison until he retired in May 1953. Sagar made his Everton debut in a 4-0 home win over Derby County in January 1930 and his last appearance in a 1-0 defeat at Plymouth Argyle in November 1952.

It was his misfortune to be a contemporary of Harry Hibbs and Vic Woodley, otherwise he would have won far more than the four England caps that came his way, the first being against Northern Ireland in October 1935. Sagar won League Championship medals with Everton in 1932 and 1939 and was between the posts when the Blues beat Manchester City 3-0 in the FA Cup Final of 1933.

Sagar combined sheer athleticism with bravery and tremendous vision. His handling, particularly of crosses, was exemplary and he survived by skill alone. He had the uncanny abiltiy to judge the high flight of the ball and was completely without nerves. Famous for launching himself headlong at the ball, regardless of the number of players blocking his path, Sagar made his farewell appearance for Everton against Tranmere Rovers in the Liverpool Senior Cup final.

Ted Sagar died on 16 October 1986 aged 76.

There were, however, some new personalities at Goodison after the war. The most impressive were Tommy Eglington and Peter Farrell, who had arrived jointly at the club from Shamrock Rovers in 1946 for £10,000. Another useful acquisition was Wally Fielding, a Charlton player before the war and who was spotted in Italy by Jack Sharp junior, a major in the Royal Ordnance Corps at Bari. There were others including Ephraim 'Jock' Dodds, who once scored a hat-trick for Blackpool in two minutes, and Eddie Wainwright, whilst another man who was to have an important influence on the club in later years also made his league debut in 1946-47 - he was a centre-forward called Harry Catterick. In that first season, Everton finished 10th with their best spell coming at the turn of the year when their six victories in the first seven matches included a 4-2 defeat of Sunderland with Eddie Wainwright netting a hat-trick. At one stage, the Blues had slipped anxiously into the relegation zone and it took a fortunate final run-in to pull themselves up to mid-table.

There was no improvement in 1947-48 as Everton dropped further down the table and finished up 14th, a position they had hovered around for much of the season. 'Jock' Dodds, who played in eight war-time internationals for Scotland, netted hat-tricks in the wins over Wolverhampton Wanderers (Away 4-2) and Huddersfield Town (Away 3-1) and topped the club's scoring charts for the second successive season. There was a rare flourish in the FA Cup as the Blues progressed to

TOMMY G. JONES

Tommy G.Jones, who was often regarded as one of the footballing 'scientists' of his day, joined Everton from Wrexham, for whom he had made just seven first team appearances, in March 1936 for a fee of £3,000.

Jones, who was a thoughtful neat player, made his debut for the Toffees some six months later in a 1-0 defeat at Leeds United but it was his only game of the season. He established himself as a first team regular in the Everton side the following season, at the end of which he won the first of his 17 Welsh caps when he played against Northern Ireland.

During the Second World War, Jones appeared in 142 games for the club and when league football resumed in 1946-47, he was again the club's first-choice pivot, scoring his first goal for the club in a 3-3 home draw against Grimsby Town.

In the summer of 1949, Jones replaced Peter Farrell as the club captain but a year earlier he could easily have left Goodison Park. Italian giants AS Roma made desperate and prolonged attempts to sign him and though Everton eventually accepted a considerable fee, the deal fell through after a row over the currency transaction.

Towards the end of his career with the Toffees, Jones upset the Everton board by publicly expressing his concerns at the way the club was being run. He had scored five goals in 175 League and Cup games when he left to join Pwllheli as the Welsh club's player-manager.

the fifth round before losing 1-0 in a replay with Fulham.

The 1948-49 season began optimistically as Cliff Britton returned to Goodison Park to take charge of team affairs, while Theo Kelly reverted to his old job as secretary. Since leaving the Blues in 1945, Britton had enjoyed a successful spell as manager of Burnley, taking the Clarets to promotion from the Second Division and to third place in the top flight.

However, the Blues made a disastrous start to the season, for after drawing 3-3 at home to Newcastle United on the opening day of the campaign, they lost their next four games without scoring a goal and went on to win just two of their opening 14 matches. One of those victories saw 'Jock' Dodds score a hat-trick in a 4-1 defeat of Preston North End. Results began to pick up after Christmas but with Dodds having left to join Lincoln City, there was no-one to score goals and it was Eddie Wainwright, who netted a hat-trick in a 5-0 rout of Blackpool, who was the club's leading scorer with 10 goals. The highlight of the season was the derby game with Liverpool which ended all-square at 1-1 but attracted a record gate to Goodison of 78,299.

At the end of the season, Everton lost the services of Alex Stevenson who had joined the club from Glasgow Rangers. The skilful inside-forward was capped 17 times by Northern Ireland and seven times by Eire in an international career that spanned 17 years.

It was to be a similar story in the league in 1949-50 as Everton again finished in eighteenth place. Wainwright was again the club's leading scorer, his total of 11 goals including a hat-trick in the 3-0 home win over Huddersfield Town. The Toffees suffered a number of heavy defeats, the worst being a 7-0 reversal at Portsmouth.

However, in the FA Cup, and against all expectations, the club reached the semi-finals. The draw for the third round saw Everton travel to Second Division Queen's Park Rangers where goals from Buckle and Catterick took them through to the next round and a tie at West Ham United. In a hard fought contest, two goals from Harry Catterick helped the Blues win 2-1 to take their place in the fifth round against the runaway Second Division leaders, Tottenham Hotspur. This time the match was at Goodison Park and though the London club were on top for much of the game, it was Everton's Eddie Wainwright who scored the only goal of the match. In the sixth round, Everton were drawn away to Derby

County where they gave a spirited performance to win 2-1 with goals from Buckle and Wainwright. With Liverpool having beaten Blackpool to clinch a place in the last four, there was great anticipation on Merseyside of an Everton-Liverpool final. But it was not to be as the two teams were drawn to play each other in the semi-final at Maine Road.

Everton started most promisingly and both Fielding and Wainwright went close, but the Blues failed to turn their domination into goals and at half-time, Liverpool led 1-0 as Bob Paisley lobbed Everton 'keeper Burnett. Early in the second-half, the Blues forced three corners in as many minutes but still had nothing to show for their efforts. Eglington came close to an equaliser but in the end Billy Liddell scored a second for the Reds to dash any hopes Everton had of reaching Wembley.

The slide into the Second Division seemed inevitable and duly arrived at the end of a disastrous 1950-51 season. Even before September was out, the club had slipped into the relegation zone and, although they pulled themselves free for a short time after a 5-1 win at Fulham in which Harry Catterick netted a hat-trick, in the spring of 1951 Everton went six matches without a goal. As the final game of the season approached, the Blues were on 32 points with both Chelsea and Sheffield Wednesday below them on 30 points. Everton, who had an inferior goal average to their rival relegation fighters, needed one more point to remain in the First Division - but in the final matches, Chelsea beat Bolton Wanderers 4-0 whilst the Blues lost 6-0 at Sheffield Wednesday - where three of the goals came in an eight-minute burst during the first-half.

It took Everton some time to settle to Second Division football and after 14 games the club had slipped to third from bottom and were staring Third Division (North) football in the face. Fortunately, results began to improve, thanks in the main to Dave Hickson and John Willie Parker. Hickson broke into the Everyon side in the early part of the season as the club's form slumped. An old-fashioned type of centre-forward, he soon became a great favourite with the Everton crowd as he hit 14 goals in 31 games. He was partnered by John Willie Parker, who top-scored with 15 goals including a hat-trick in a 5-0 home win over Hull City, helping the Toffees finish the season in seventh place.

There was no improvement in 1952-53 and after losing their opening three games of the season, Everton found themselves bottom of Division Two. That situation was rectified in the fifth game of the campaign when the Blues defeated Nottingham Forest 3-0 and on 27 September, Tommy Eglington scored five of the team's goals in a 7-1 rout of Doncaster Rovers. Despite wins agaisnt Bury (Away 5-0), where Harry Potts scored a hat-trick, and Brentford (Home 5-0), with Dave Hickson netting a treble, Everton were always in danger of slipping back down towards the relegation zone. After an 8-2 defeat at Huddersfield Town in early April, there were more than a few Everton supporters who would have bet on

WALLY FIELDING

Before he joined the Army, Wally Fielding was on Charlton Athletic's books as an amateur. When he left the Army in 1945, he was immediately offered terms by Charlton, who naturally assumed they had first refusal. But despite the attention of a number of other leading clubs, he opted for Theo Kelly's Everton and started a furious debate which lasted for months.

Fielding made his league debut for the Toffees in a 2-0 home defeat by Brentford in the opening game of the 1946-47 season. He made the Number 10 shirt his own over the next twelve years, appearing in 410 League and Cup games for the Goodison club.

One of Fielding's trademarks was his perfectly weighted passes inside the full-back to Tommy Eglington. He was certainly more than capable of looking after himself in the face of the most ferocious tackles, running the Everton engine-room with great authority.

Though never a prolific marksman, he posssessed a powerful and accurate shot and netted 54 goals in his Goodison career.

Dubbed as 'Merseyside's answer to Len Shackleton', he made only one appearance in the white shirt of England, that being in the Bolton Disaster Fund game against Scotland at Manchester in 1946, a game that did not count as an official full cap.

Fielding was a chirpy character and a most positive influence on the Everton youngsters, who used to copy his mannerism of clutching his rolled-down shirt-sleeves as he ran. He was nearing 40 when he left Goodison Park for Southport in 1959 but, still bubbling with enthusiasm, he managed twenty league games for the Sandgrounders.

them dropping into the Third Division but somehow they clung on and finished the season in 16th place, five points clear of relegation.

In the FA Cup, the Blues surprised everyone by going all the way to the semi-final. Drawn at home in the third round, they found the extra-class needed to beat Ipswich Town of Division Three 3-2. The next round brought Second Division Nottingham Forest to Goodison and they were comfortably beaten 4-1. A crowd of 77,920 turned up for the fifth round tie against League champions Manchester United. After Jack Rowley had given United an early lead, Eglington equalised for the Blues before Dave Hickson, with blood pouring out of an open-head wound caused by an earlier injury, scored the winner with just 15 minutes remaining. In the quarter-finals, Everton travelled to Villa Park to meet an Aston Villa side led by the skilful and imaginative Danny Blanchflower.

With time running out and a goalless draw looking likely, Dave Hickson slid home Ted Buckle's carefully-weighted pass for the game's only goal. In the semi-final, Everton faced Bolton Wanderers at Maine Road, a ground where on three previous occasions at this stage of the competition the Blues had lost!

By half-time, the game looked to be as good as over as Everton trooped off dejectedly 4-0 down. Two of the Bolton goals had been scored by the 'Lion of Vienna', Nat Lofthouse, as the then Burnden Park side ran Everton ragged. The Blues cause hadn't been helped by the fact that they lost Dave Hickson with a head injury for 15 minutes midway through the first-half and then, on the stroke of half-time, Clinton missed a penalty after Hartle had handled. But the second-half was a different story and within a minute of the restart, Parker had pulled one back. Peter Farrell added a second from a twice-taken free-kick and then, with six minutes remaining, Parker headed home Everton's third goal. Suddenly it was Bolton who were reeling but although they threw everything at the Wanderers, Everton could not complete what would have been an epic recovery.

The cup run had obviously done Everton's confidence a power of good for they started the 1953-54 season with a run of eleven games without defeat, the first of which came in a 1-0 reversal at Brentford on 3 October. Hickson and Parker were now playing with real flair and both

8

scored hat-tricks in the early part of the season, Parker in a 3-1 home win over Oldham Athletic and Hickson in a 4-2 victory at Stoke City. In February 1954, the Toffees scored twenty goals in three consecutive games - Derby County (Away 6-2), Brentford (Home 6-1) and Plymouth Argyle (Home 8-4). In this last match, John Willie Parker, who topped the scoring charts with 31 goals in 38 games, netted four of Everton's goals. The Blues needed to win their last match at Oldham to win promotion - they did so 4-0 and ended the season as runners-up to Leicester City on goal average.

The final table was as follows:

	P.	W.	D.	L.	F.	A.	Pts
Leicester City	42	25	11	6	109	67	61
Everton	42	20	16	6	92	58	56
Blackburn Rovers	42	23	9	10	86	50	55

During the club's first season back in the top flight, they were drawn against Liverpool in the fourth round of the FA Cup. With the Reds wallowing in the lower reaches of the Second Division, the result looked a foregone conclusion. However, the Reds had something to prove and in front of a Goodison Park crowd of 72,000 trounced Everton 4-0.

The Blues had won their first fixture back in the top flight, 5-2 at Sheffield United, and in fact won four of their first five matches. However, they fell away and during the course of the season suffered successive 5-0 defeats in the games at Portsmouth and Charlton Athletic and ended the campaign in 11th place.

In 1955-56, Everton's form declined and they ended the season in 15th place. Results were mixed with the Christmas matches against Birmingham City highlighting the club's plight. On Christmas Day the Blues travelled to St Andrew's and were well beaten 6-2 but in the return at Goodison on Boxing Day, Everton triumphed 5-1. However, they clearly missed Dave Hickson, who, disgruntled at Jimmy Harris's liking for his shirt, was transferred to Aston Villa for £17,500. Harris did well, scoring 21 League and Cup goals in his first season with the club. In that season's FA Cup, the Blues reached the quarter-finals before going out 2-1 to Manchester City at Maine Road.

During the summer, the team were on tour with manager Cliff Britton when the club decided to announce that it was appointing an acting-manager. Britton, who knew nothing of the decision, was so angry that he resigned immediately. Two months later, Ian Buchan, the one-time Scottish amateur international and former Loughborough College lecturer, was appointed to take charge of team affairs. Buchan was a fitness fanatic and demanded the same sort of commitment from his players.

In his first game in charge at the start of the 1956-57 season, he stopped the team coach two miles short of the Leeds United ground and

TOMMY EGLINGTON

One of Everton's greatest-ever servants, Tommy Eglington missed very few games for the Toffees in the eleven years immediately after the Second World War, scoring 82 goals in 428 League and Cup appearances.

Eglington joined Everton, along with Peter Farrell, from Shamrock Rovers in 1946 for a joint fee of £10,000, the deal proving to be one of the best strokes of business that the Goodison club has ever pulled off.

He made his league debut for Everton in a 3-2 home win over Arsenal in September 1946. Eglington's speed and trickery earned him 24 full caps for the Republic of Ireland and another six for Northern Ireland. He appeared alongside Peter Farrell in the historic game at Goodison Park in 1949 when the Republic of Ireland defeated England 2-0 to become the first 'overseas' nation to win on English soil.

Eglington guaranteed himself a place in the pages of Everton history when on 27 September 1952, he almost single-handedly demolished Doncaster Rovers at Goodison Park by scoring five goals in a 7-1 win. A player with intricate close control and stunning shooting power, the very mention of Eglington's name sent shivers of apprehension down the spines of right-backs up and down the country.

Tommy Eglington left Everton for Tranmere Rovers in 1957, and though during his time at Prenton Park he was more of a goal-maker than a goalscorer, he did net a hat-trick in a 5-1 win over Accrington Stanley. After Rovers had been relegated in 1960-61, Eglington, who had scored 40 goals in 181 games for Tranmere, returned to his native Dublin to run a butcher's shop.

PETER FARRELL

Peter Farrell's career coincided with that of Tommy Eglington. They both arrived at Goodison Park from Shamrock Rovers in the summer of 1946 and Farrell too joined Tranmere Rovers as player-manager in October 1957, four months after Eglington had joined the Prenton Park club.

The Dublin-born wing-half was only one of a handful of players to appear in full internationals for both Northern Ireland and the Republic of Ireland. He represented Northern Ireland on seven occasions when they could select players born in the Republic for the Home International Championship. He won the first two of his 28 caps for the Republic of Ireland after the Second World War when he was still playing for Shamrock Rovers, and his first while with Everton against Spain in 1947. In 1949 he helped to make history when he scored one of the goals for the Republic of Ireland against England at Goodison Park. The Republic became the first non-British team to defeat England at home.

Farrell was a resilient player who never ever shirked a tackle and was popular with the fans both on and off the field, mixing freely with the club's supporters in a down-to-earth manner.

Farrell captained the Toffees for a number of years and in eleven seasons at Goodison Park scored 17 goals in 453 League and Cup games.

His spell at Tranmere was not the happiest of experiences and after posts with Wrexham and Holyhead, he returned to Ireland to continue in management.

made the players walk the rest of the way! Leeds won 5-1 and in the next three games, the Blues' defence leaked ten more goals and conceded five goals or more on five occasions in that campaign. It was not a good start and after failing to win in their opening seven games, the Blues quickly slipped into the relegation zone.

However, when Everton visited Old Trafford to play champions Manchester United, who had gone 26 games without defeat, they won an astonishing game 5-2. A week later they beat Arsenal 4-0 and later in the season Charlton Athletic 5-0, but sandwiched in between were a 6-0

TOMMY E. JONES

Liverpool-born Tommy E.Jones was Everton's first-choice centre-half throughout the 1950s. He signed professional forms after successfully captaining the England and Liverpool County FA Youth teams. Jones was originally a full-back but Everton manager Cliff Britton recognised his potential and converted him into a centre-half when the Toffees needed a replacement for his namesake Tommy G.Jones. He made his senior debut in a 2-1 defeat at Arsenal in September 1950 and, though he was a strong tackler and powerful in the air, he lacked the streak of ruthlessness that runs through most top defenders.

Cool and unruffled he excelled in clashes with Bolton Wanderers and England centre-forward Nat Lofthouse.

Full international honours surprisingly eluded him but he did play for an England XI against the British Army at Maine Road and captained the FA side that toured Ghana and Nigeria in the summer of 1958.

A cool converter of penalty-kicks, Jones became Everton's captain on Peter Farrell's departure in 1957. Eventually the slowness on the turn which had always been in evidence grew more marked, and after David Herd had netted four times for Arsenal in a 6-1 win for the Gunners at Goodison in September 1958, he was replaced by the young Brian Labone.

Jones' career came to an end after he smashed his knee-cap in a Central League game at Barnsley. In the early 1960s, he left Britain to coach Italian club Montreal.

defeat at Tottenham Hotspur on Christmas Day and a 5-1 reversal at Aston Villa. At the end of the season in which Everton again finished 15th, they lost the services of Tommy Eglington and captain Peter Farrell, the pair of them joining Tranmere Rovers.

Everton started the 1957-58 season in fine style, losing just one of their opening twelve fixtures but after beating Newcastle United 3-2 on 12 October 1957, didn't win another game until Boxing Day when they won 5-1 at Bolton Wanderers! It was around this time that Eddie Thomas was introduced into the Blues' first team and he responded with 15 goals in 29 games, including all four in the 4-2 defeat of Preston North End, helping Everton finish the season in 16th place.

A Concise Post-War History of Everton

After losing the first six matches of the 1958-59 season, the Everton board decided that Ian Buchan was not going to lead them to glory and appointed former Manchester United captain Johnny Carey as their manager. Just prior to his appointment, the club had re-signed Bobby Collins from Celtic for a staggering £23,500. The deal was made possible thanks to the introduction of pools millionaire John Moores to the Everton boardroom. Moores, who had founded the football pools empire of

DAVE HICKSON

Dave Hickson first attracted the attention of Toffees' manager Cliff Britton as a free-scoring teenager with Ellesmere Port, but after crossing the Mersey to join the Goodison Park club in the summer of 1948, his progress was halted by National Service. Two years later he returned to an Everton side that had been relegated to the Second Division and made his debut in a 2-1 win at Leeds United in September 1951. He soon claimed a regular place in the Toffees' line-up, linking effectively with John Willie Parker.

He earned himself a place in Everton folklore during the club's run to the 1953 FA Cup semi-finals when in the fifth round tie with Manchester United he scored the winner after leaving the field to have five stitches inserted in a gashed eyebrow. The wound later reopened when Hickson thudded a header against the United upright. In the quarter-final at Villa Park he scored the only goal of the game with a powerful drive from just inside the penalty area after starting the move near the halfway line.

During the 1953-54 season, when he scored 25 league goals, he netted his first hat-trick for the club in a 4-2 win at Stoke City. After losing his place to Jimmy Harris, he was transferred to Aston Villa for £17,500 but on failing to settle in the Midlands, he moved to Huddersfield Town two months later for £16,000. In July 1957 he returned to Goodison for a bargain £7,500 but after taking his tally of goals to 111 in 243 games, he was allowed to cross Stanley Park and join Liverpool.

Twelve months later he left Anfield and went into non-League football with Cambridge United. Though he later had a stint with Tranmere Rovers, there is never any doubt about where his heart lay - Dave Hickson was and is an Everton man through and through.

15

Littlewoods, had always been an Everton fan and within two years would be chairman and leading the club into a new era.

However, despite Carey's appointment, results were slow to pick up and on 11 October 1958, Everton, who were bottom of the First Division, suffered the biggest defeat in their history when Tottenham Hotspur beat them 10-4 at White Hart Lane. Jimmy Harris netted a hat-trick for the Blues and Everton's four goals were the highest away score in the League that day but that was little consolation! Carey began to introduce new faces into the team, notably Albert Dunlop, Brian Labone and new signing Alex Parker. They helped to strengthen the defence and by the end of the season, Everton had managed to finish 16th.

BRIAN HARRIS

Bebington-born Brian Harris was one of the club's greatest-ever utility players, having played in every position except goalkeeper for the Everton first team.

Harris was a winger when he joined the Blues from Port Sunlight in January 1954 but he had to wait until August 1955 before making his first team debut in a 1-0 win at Burnley. Over the next twelve seasons, he went on to score 29 goals in 358 League and Cup games, winning a League Championship medal in 1962-63 and an FA Cup winners' medal in 1966 when he was one of Everton's best players in the 3-2 win over Sheffield Wednesday. Best remembered as a defensive wing-half, he was a great favourite with the Goodison faithful, and therefore it came as a great surprise in October 1966 when he was allowed to join Cardiff City for a fee of £15,000.

He made his debut for the Bluebirds in a 7-1 defeat at Plymouth Argyle, the first of 149 league appearances Harris made for the Ninian Park club. In 1967-68 he played in all nine of the Welsh club's European Cup Winners' Cup games when they just missed out on reaching the final. Harris left Cardiff City in the summer of 1971 to become player-manager of Newport County. He made 85 appearances for the Somerton Park club and almost led them to promotion in 1972 but later resigned after a disagreement with the board over finances. Harris later returned to Ninian Park as assistant-manager to Richie Morgan, a post he held for two years.

JIMMY HARRIS

Birkenhead-born Jimmy Harris was a member of the district's successful schoolboy team before joining the Goodison Park club as an amateur. After making the transition to the club's professional ranks, he made his debut for the Toffees in a 1-0 win at Burnley in August 1955, replacing Dave Hickson. Harris kept his place in the side, appearing in all 40 remaining games and top-scoring with 23 League and Cup goals. Midway through that season, he won England Under-23 honours when he played against Scotland at Hillsborough. When Hickson, who had joined Aston Villa, returned to Goodison from his new club, Huddersfield Town, in the summer of 1957, Harris switched from centre-forward to outside-right but still continued to score more goals than the fomer Everton favourite.

In October 1958, Harris scored a hat-trick in the match against Tottenham Hotspur at White Hart Lane but still ended up on the losing side as the Toffees went down 10-4. In December 1960, after scoring 72 goals in 207 League and Cup games, he left Goodison to join Birmingham City for a 'substantial' fee.

His first league game for the St Andrew's club was against the Toffees, an entertaining game which Everton won 4-3. Harris ended his first season with his new club as top scorer with 13 goals. He repeated the feat in 1961-62 and went on in four seasons with the club to score 53 goals in 115 outings. His only honour while with Birmingham was a League Cup winners' tankard in 1962-63 as Aston Villa were beaten in the two-legged final. In July 1964 he joined Oldham Athletic, moving to Tranmere Rovers two years later. Unable to break into the Prenton Park club's first team, he hung up his boots.

The club finished 16th again the following season after failing to win any of their opening six games. Their first success came on 16 September when two goals from Dave Hickson helped the Toffees beat Blackburn Rovers 2-0. Everton were very much an up-and-down side in 1959-60. At the end of October they beat Leicester City 6-1 only to lose 8-2 at Newcastle United a week later! In their next match the Blues beat Birmingham City 4-0 with Alan Shackleton netting a hat-trick. Everton had some good home wins, beating both Nottingham Forest and Chelsea 6-1. However, they failed to win an away game all season, losing 6-2 at

West Bromwich Albion and 5-0 at Manchester United on the final day of the campaign.

After a hesitant start to the 1960-61 season, Everton embarked on a 13-match unbeaten run, playing some impeccable football. In the last of those matches, the Blues beat Newcastle United 5-0 with Bobby Collins netting a hat-trick. Carey began to develop an accomplished side, adding to the ranks all the time. New signings Billy Bingham, from Luton Town, and Alex Young, from Heart of Midlothian for £55,000, soon made their mark. By the turn of the year, the Blues were in second place behind Tottenham Hotspur but four successive defeats as one of the coldest winters gripped the country saw them slide down the table. The frozen pitches were not to the liking of the Blues' delicate ball-playing skills but as the weather improved, results began to pick up. Collins netted another hat-trick in a 5-1 defeat of Cardiff and Roy Vernon, who

DEREK TEMPLE

Having played for Lancashire and England Schoolboys, Liverpool-born Derek Temple joined Everton shortly after leaving school.

His form with the Everton Colts side was amazing; in one season alone he scored 70 goals, including six in one match and five on a number of occasions. His form was such that he soon made his first team debut for the Toffees, starring in a 2-1 win over Newcastle United in March 1957. He played in seven games at the end of that season, scoring three goals including one in his second game, a 2-2 draw at Sheffield Wednesday.

In 1965 he was capped by England, playing against West Germany in Nuremberg, a match the English won 1-0.

The following season he won a place in Everton's 'Hall of Fame' when he scored the winning goal in the Toffees' marvellous 3-2 win over Sheffield Wednesday in the FA Cup Final at Wembley.

Temple went on to score 82 goals in 273 League and Cup games for Everton, including a hat-trick in a 5-2 defeat of Ipswich Town in September 1961.

In September 1967, he was transferred to Preston North End for £35,000, playing in a variety of roles. In three seasons at Deepdale, Temple scored 14 goals in 76 league games before leaving to see out his career with non-League Wigan Athletic.

ended the season as the club's leading scorer with 21 goals, finished the campaign with a hat-trick in a 4-1 win over Arsenal. The Toffees ended the season in fifth place in the First Division, their best post-war position to date.

The 1960-61 season was also the inaugural season of the League Cup. The Blues progressed to the fifth round after Frank Wignall had hit a hat-trick in a 4-0 win at Tranmere Rovers but went out of the competition after losing 2-1 at Shrewsbury Town.

Johnny Carey had done well, pulling the Blues out of their long post-war depression but John Moores felt that he lacked the hunger and dedication to make Everton League Champions again. It was in the back of a London taxi that Moores broke the news to Carey, telling the former Irish international that his short career at Goodison was over.

It didn't take long for the Everton board to appoint a replacement. Former Blues' centre-forward Harry Catterick had been managing Sheffield Wednesday, taking the Owls into the First Division and to second place within a year.

Under Catterick, the Blues began the 1961-62 season very nervously and though Derek Temple netted a hat-trick in a 5-2 defeat of Ipswich Town, they lost six games before the end of September and found themselves in the relegation zone. Catterick reorganised the defence, after which the Blues lost just one game out of 14 before the turn of the year. They included a 6-0 win over Nottingham Forest and a 5-1 thrashing of Manchester United. Mid-way through the season he sold Bobby Collins to Leeds United. Collins had scored 48 goals in 147 games for Everton and had always given of his best. His replacement was Dennis Stevens from Bolton Wanderers, whilst also arriving at Goodison Park was Blackpool 'keeper Gordon West, who cost £27,500, a record fee for a goalkeeper. The Blues, who were unbeaten in their last nine matches, beat Cardiff City 8-3 with Roy Vernon, who was the club's leading scorer with 28 goals, netting a hat-trick. Everton ended the season in fourth place, just five points behind champions Ipswich Town.

The 1962-63 season got off to just the start the Blues were hoping for with four successive wins taking the club to the top of Division One for the first time since May 1939. With only two games of the campaign played, Catterick signed winger Johnny Morrissey from Liverpool for

BRIAN LABONE

One of the greatest players to wear the royal blue of Everton, Brian Labone won every honour in the game, including 26 England caps, and captained the club for seven years. He made his Everton debut in a 2-1 defeat at Birmingham City in March 1958 but after being given the runaround by Bobby Smith in a 4-3 win for the Spurs the following week, he was dropped.

The following season he replaced the injured Tommy E.Jones and stayed in the side until 1971, when an Achilles injury ended his career.

During the 1962-63 season he became the first Everton player to be capped since the war and was a great influence on the club's League Championship-winning campaign. After holding aloft the FA Cup in 1966, he asked to be excused from England's World Cup party to concentrate on his wedding plans and in 1967 astounded the football world by announcing his retirement! Having lost both form and confidence, Labone told the Everton board that he would part company with them in eighteen months time, or as soon as a suitable replacement had been found, to enable him to enter his family business. Thankfully he changed his mind and he soon returned to peak form. Alf Ramsey continued to pick him at international level and in 1969-70 he won another League Championship medal.

After injurying his Achilles tendon in a Central League game in September 1971, he was forced to quit the game the following year. He had scored two goals in 530 League and Cup games for the Toffees. Honoured at Goodison Park as a loyal and distinguished player, he was, as Harry Catterick once called him, 'the last of the great Corinthians'.

£10,000 and he had a hand in all Everton's goals on his debut as Sheffield Wednesday were beaten 4-1. On 22 September 1962, Morrissey lined up against his former club at Goodison Park for what was the first League derby since January 1951. A crowd of 72,488 saw Roy Vernon give the Blues the lead from the penalty-spot but Kevin Lewis equalised for Luverpool just before half-time. Johnny Morrissey netted his first goal for the club mid-way through the second-half but with the referee poised to blow for full-time, Roger Hunt levelled things up for the Anfield side. In Everton's next game, Morrissey, in only his

ninth appearance for the club, scored a hat-trick in a 4-2 defeat of West Bromwich Albion.

Just after the turn of the year, Catterick made two important additions to the Everton squad in the shape of Glasgow Rangers' winger Alex Scott for £40,000 and Sheffield Wednesday half-back Tony Kay for £55,000. Everton, like all other league clubs, had just endured the bitterest winter in recent memory, not playing a league game between 22 December 1962 and 12 February 1963, although they did play a couple of FA Cup ties. When the Blues' league programme got back underway, they found themselves in second place to Tottenham Hotspur. Undefeated in their last twelve league games of the season, Everton wrapped up the League Championship in their final game of the campaign, with Roy Vernon netting a hat-trick in a 4-1 hammering of Fulham. Vernon was again the club's leading marksman with 24 goals in 41 games, whilst Alex Young had 22 in 42 matches. The League Championship trophy was paraded around Goodison and for the first time since 1939, the cry of 'Champions' could be heard!

The final placings were as follows:

	P.	W.	D.	L.	F.	A.	Pts
Everton	42	25	11	6	84	42	61
Tottenham Hotspur	42	23	9	10	111	62	55
Burnley	42	22	10	10	78	57	54

In the FA Cup, the Blues won 3-0 at Barnsley and 5-1 at Swindon Town before losing to West Ham United in round five, the Hammers winning by the only goal of the game at Upton Park.

Everton's fourth spot in Division One the previous season entitled them to a place in the Inter Cities Fairs Cup. For their opening game in the competition, they drew Scottish opposition in Dunfermlione Athletic. The Blues won the first leg at Goodison Park 1-0, with Dennis Stevens the Everton scorer, but surprisingly lost the return game in Scotland 2-0 to go out of the competition at the first hurdle!

However, as League Champions, the following season would see the Blues involved in the most coveted of all European trophies, the European Cup.

Everton began the 1963-64 season where they'd let off, beating

Fulham 3-0 on the opening day of the campaign. But the following week they were brought firmly down to earth as Manchester United beat them 5-1 at Old Trafford. It was a defeat from which the team suffered a complete loss of confidence, yet just two weeks after, they were facing Italian champions Inter Milan in the first round of the European Cup. The first leg at Goodison was goalless as the visitors erected a defensive wall and sat back contentedly and soaked up the pressure. In the return leg at the San Siro Stadium, manager Harry Catterick was forced to give a debut to 18-year-old Colin Harvey as Jimmy Gabriel was injured. The young midfielder had an outstanding game but in a stadium packed with

BOBBY COLLINS

Bobby Collins joined the Toffees straight from Scottish junior football but was desperately homesick and after only a few weeks returned north of the border to sign for Glasgow Celtic. In 1951 he won the first of 31 caps for Scotland when he played against Wales.

In 1958 Collins left Parkhead and rejoined the Blues for a fee of £39,000. He made a goalscoring debut in a 3-1 win over Manchester City at Maine Road only hours after putting pen to paper. The diminutive player - standing just 5ft 4ins and weighing 10st 3lbs - was the Toffees' leading scorer in 1959-60 with 14 goals. He scored 16 goals the following season, a total that included hat-tricks in the wins over Newcastle United (Home 5-0) and Cardiff City (Home 5-1). In March 1962, after scoring 48 goals in 147 League and Cup games, he was surprisingly allowed to leave Goodison Park and joined Leeds United for £30,000.

Many saw it as a backward step, especially as the Yorkshire club seemed destined to be relegated to the Third Division. However, over the next three seasons the Elland Road club won promotion and narrowly missed a League and Cup double. Despite breaking a thigh bone in an Inter Cities Fairs Cup match in Turin, Collins went on to play in over 150 games for Leeds before joining Bury on a free transfer in 1967. After a spell back in Scotland with Morton, he coached in both Australia and South Africa before becoming player-coach of Oldham Athletic. He later had spells in charge at Hull City, Huddersfield Town and Barnsley.

90,000 fanatical supporters, the Blues were always going to be up against it and went down 1-0.

Back in the League, Everton lost 2-1 to Liverpool at Anfield and slipped into the bottom half of the First Division. In November, the Blues participated in the newly created British Championship, beating Glasgow Rangers 3-1 at Goodison and drawing 1-1 at Ibrox Park to take the trophy.

After beating Burnley 3-2 at Turf Moor, the Blues went twelve games without defeat, including beating Nottingham Forest 6-1 with new signing Fred Pickering netting a hat-trick on his home debut. Sadly, after getting themselves back into contention for the League Championship, the

JIMMY GABRIEL

When Jimmy Gabriel joined Everton from Dundee in March 1960 for a fee of £30,000, he became one of the most expensive teenagers in British football. Within 72 hours of putting pen to paper, Gabriel had made his debut for the Blues in a 2-2 draw at West Ham United. He went on to build a fine career for himself, scoring 36 goals in 301 games for the Toffees.

A powerhouse of a right-half, he was the perfect foil for the adventurous wanderings of Brian Harris at left-half. An ever-present in 1961-62, he played a major part in the club's League Championship success the following season and was a member of the Everton side that won the FA Cup in 1966.

Gabriel moved to the south coast to play for Southampton in the summer of 1967. In five seasons at the Dell, Gabriel notched up nearly 200 appearances and when he left for Bournemouth in July 1972 his presence was sorely missed. After leaving Dean Court, Gabriel had brief spells with Swindon Town and Brentford before moving to North America where he played for Seattle Sounders.

He returned to Goodison Park in the summer of 1990 to help manager Colin Harvey look after the first team, later taking over as caretaker boss before Howard Kendall's second coming. Since then he has remained part of the Goodison club's coaching set-up, but it's as an accomplished top-flight performer when the Toffees had their backs to the wall that Everton fans will forever remember Jimmy Gabriel.

Blues fell away, losing three of their last five matches. They finished the campaign in third place, five points adrift of the champions Liverpool!

Towards the end of the season, Everton captain Tony Kay, along with Sheffield Wednesday's Peter Swan and 'Bronco' Lyne, were alleged to have thrown a game involving the Owls and Ipswich Town. As soon as the revelations broke, the Everton board suspended Kay, though there was never any suggestion that he had fixed a game whilst with the Blues. When the allegations came to came to court in October 1964, Kay was sentenced to four months imprisonment and banned from football for life.

During the summer, Everton signed Huddersfield Town full-back Ray Wilson and he lined-up in the Blues' side at Stoke on the opening day of the 1964-65 season. Goals from Temple and Vernon gave Everton

ROY VERNON

Roy Vernon had the chance to go to Goodison Park as a schoolboy but he turned down the opportunity and eventually turned professional with Blackburn Rovers. The Welsh international won the first nine caps of his total of 32 as a Rovers player and although he didn't realise it at the time, he robbed himself of a Wembley appearance when he finally became an Everton player in February 1960.

It was Johnny Carey, his former manager at Ewood Park, who lured him to Goodison in a £27,500 deal which took Eddie Thomas to Blackburn in part-exchange.

He made his Everton debut in a 2-0 home defeat at the hands of Wolverhampton Wanderers, going on to score nine goals in the final 12 games of the season. In 1960-61 he was the club's leading scorer with 21 goals including a hat-trick in a 4-1 win over Arsenal on the final day of the season. In 1961-62 he was again the club's top scorer with 26 goals in 37 league outings, including another treble in an 8-3 rout of Cardiff City. Vernon set about his work with compelling efficiency and skippered the side to the League title in 1962-63, netting another hat-trick in a 4-1 win over Fulham as the Toffees clinched the title. Vernon went on to score 110 goals in 199 League and Cup games before moving to Stoke City in March 1965.

When he lost his place in the Stoke side after five productive years with the Potters, he moved to Halifax Town where he ended his league career.

a 2-0 win and this was followed by victories over Nottingham Forest (Home 1-0) and Tottenham Hotspur (Home 4-1). In this latter match Fred Pickering netted a hat-trick, proving to be worth every penny of his £85,000 transfer fee. During the course of the season the Blues went twelve consecutive matches without defeat and, with Pickering top-scoring with 27 league goals, they finished fourth, some twelve points behind champions Manchester United.

In the FA Cup, Everton went out in the fourth round to Leeds United, whom they had held to a 1-1 draw at Elland Road before being beaten 2-1 at Goodison. In the Inter Cities Fairs Cup, Everton beat Valerengens IF of Spain 5-2 in the first leg before a 4-2 victory at Goodison gave the Blues a comprehensive aggregate victory. In the second round, Everton travelled to Scotland to take on Kilmarnock and established a 2-0 lead to take into the second leg. Fred Pickering netted twice at Goodison in a 4-1 win to take the Blues into the third round where they were drawn against Manchester United. A crowd of 60,000 witnessed the first leg at Old Trafford where Fred Pickering scored in a 1-1 draw. Hopes were high for the return leg but despite Pickering scoring again for the Blues, United's attack exploited the gaps left by the defenders and won 2-1. Fred Pickering's arrival - he scored 37 League and Cup goals in 1964-65 - led to the departure of Roy Vernon to Stoke City.

Despite beating Northampton Town 5-2 on the opening day of the 1965-66 season and Sheffield Wednesday 5-1 in the fourth game with Alex Young netting a hat-trick, the Blues' league form left a lot to be desired. On 25 September 1965, they were thrashed 5-0 by Liverpool, though they did regain a little pride with a goalless home draw against the Reds later in the season. It was a fairly unmemorable league campaign and as the various cup competitions took their toll, the Blues finished the season in seventh place.

In the Inter Cities Fairs Cup, Everton drew 1-1 with IFC Nuremberg in Germany thanks to a Brian Harris goal, whilst in the return match at Goodison, Jimmy Gabriel scored the only goal of the game. In the second round they visited Ujpest Dozsa of Hungary, but after losing the first leg 3-0 they were always going to be up against it and, despite winning the return leg at Goodison 2-1, they went out of the competition 4-2 on aggregate.

The Toffees

In that season's FA Cup, goals from Pickering, Temple and Young gave the Blues a third round win over Sunderland and set up a fourth round meeting with non-League Bedford Town. On a small, sloping pitch, Derek Temple netted twice in a 3-0 win. The fifth round draw paired the Blues with high-flying Second Division club, Coventry City. Again the Blues won 3-0 with Pickering, Temple and Young the goalscorers. In the quarter-finals, Everton again faced Second Division opposition in Manchester City. So far nobody had managed to score against the Blues and after a goalless draw at Maine Road the teams replayed at Everton, a match which again failed to produce a goal. In the second replay at Molineux, Pickering and Temple kept up their record of having scored in every round as the Blues came away with a 2-0 win. Through to their third semi-final since the war, the Blues faced

FRED PICKERING

One of Everton's finest post-war strikers, Fred Pickering began his career as a full-back with Blackburn Rovers. He had enjoyed success in the Ewood Park club's junior teams, helping to win the FA Youth Cup in 1959, but when he was given a chance in the first team, he failed to impress. Rovers manager Jack Marshall decided to gamble with him at centre-forward after some powerful displays in that position with the reserves. He had the happy knack of putting the ball in the net and soon began to create a name for himself. In fact, he became so prolific, scoring 59 goals in 123 league games for Rovers, that when Harry Catterick's £85,000 bid was accepted, there was outrage in Blackburn.

Pickering signalled his arrival on Merseyside with a hat-trick on his debut as Nottingham Forest were beaten 6-1. Two mopnths later he scored another hat-trick in his first match for England as the United States were beaten 10-0 in New York. Pickering's best season was 1964-65, when he scored 37 goals in 51 League and Cup games including another treble in a 4-1 home win over Tottenham Hotspur. The following season Pickering suffered a cartilage problem and had to miss Everton's FA Cup semi-final victory over Manchester United. Though he declared himself fit for the final against Sheffield Wednesday, manager Catterick had his doubts about his ability to last ninety minutes and did not select him. His days seemed to be numbered and, after scoring 68 goals in 107 games for the Toffees, he was allowed to join Birmingham City for £50,000. He later returned to the north-west to play for Blackpool in 1969 but after helping the Seasiders win promotion, he returned to Ewood Park. Rovers boss Ken Furphy later released him, claiming he was out of condition.

Manchester United at Burnden Park, the home of Bolton Wanderers. Everton soaked up an awful lot of pressure from the champions but counter-attacked to great effect with Colin Harvey shooting them into the final where their opponents were Sheffield Wednesday.

FA Cup Final 1966: Everton 3 Sheffield Wednesday 2

Blues' manager Harry Catterick decided to axe Goodison favourite Fred Pickering and replace him with young Cornishman Mike Trebilcock, a relatively unknown striker signed for £20,000 from

29

Plymouth Argyle the previous New Year's Eve.

Wednesday took the lead after only four minutes when Jim McCalliog's shot took a defelction off Ray Wilson and wrong footed Gordon West in the Everton goal. Midway through the first-half, Ron Springett, Wednesday's England international 'keeper, brought down Alex Young but Everton's claims for a penalty were waved away. Wednesday went further ahead in the 57th minute when David Ford drove home after West had parried Fantham's shot.

Two minutes after the Owls' second goal, Trebilcock's right-foot shot reduced the arrears and five minutes later, the Blues were level when the Cornishman netted his and Everton's second goal after Alex Scott's free-kick had only been partly cleared. With just ten minutes to play, Gerry

ALEX YOUNG

Alex Young was one of the most talked about players of his generation. He arrived at Goodison Park in November 1960 along with his Hearts team-mate Georghe Thomson. When he arrived on Merseyside he was carrying a knee injury and so had to wait until December before making his debut in a 3-1 home defeat at the hands of Tottenham Hotspur. Alex Young was majestic in the air - his timing was so exquisite that he seemed to hover.

During the club's League Championship-winning season of 1962-63, Young scored 22 goals and laid on many more for leading goalscorer Roy Vernon. He knew instinctively where to play the ball and was always well aware of all the options around him without having to look up. To accompany his flair and grace, Young possessed a vicious shot as well as great heading ability. Surprisingly for all his skill and natural ability, Young only made eight appearances for Scotland, the first againt England in 1960 whilst still with Hearts.

His blond hair made him a distinctive figure on the field of play and the fans called him the 'Golden Vision' - an inspired nickname.

In August 1968, Alex Young, who had scored 87 goals in 271 League and Cup games for the Toffees, became player-manager of Glentoran. However, after only two months in charge, he joined Stockport County. Unfortunately he was forced into retirement with knee trouble, having played in only 23 games for the Edgeley Park club.

JOHNNY MORRISSEY

Winger Johnny Morrissey arrived at Goodison Park from neighbours Liverpool for a bargain fee of £10,000 in September 1962. After making his Everton debut in a 4-1 home win over Sheffield Wednesday, and having a hand in three of the goals, he quickly established himself as a first team regular. In his seventh game, he scored his first goal for the Toffees in a 2-2 draw against Liverpool in the Merseyside derby.

Although he didn't score too many goals himself - 50 in his 314 League and Cup games - he did score the all-important dramatic winner from the penalty-spot against Leeds United in the 1968 FA Cup semi-final at Old Trafford. Unfortunately he had to be satisfied with a runners-up medal as the Toffees lost 1-0 to West Bromwich Albion in the final.

In 1969-70, when Everton won the League Championship, Morrissey played in all but one game, creating many of Joe Royle's 23 goals. Two seasons later, though, Morrissey found his first team place under threat and left Goodison to play for Oldham Athletic.

Sadly, he had made just six league appearances for the Boundary Park club before injury forced his retirement from the game.

GORDON WEST

Gordon West began his Football League career with Blackpool, making his debut for the Seasiders as a 17-year-old at Bolton in January 1961. In March 1962, Everton manager Harry Catterick paid £27,000 to secure West's services, his first signing as the Toffees' boss. It was then a record fee for a goalkeeper and it paid immediate dividends as West replaced Albert Dunlop and helped the Blues take the League Championship in his first full season with the club.

West was an instinctive performer and courageous at close-quarter blocks; he was also a breathtaking shot-stopper. One weakness that the Everton 'keeper did possess was a rather inadequate kick - a legacy of a long-standing thigh injury, but the talented goalkeeper compensated amply with constructive throws in the manner of Manchester City's Bert Trautmann. In his first two seasons with the Toffees, West shared the goalkeeping duties with Andy Rankin. After that he missed only a handful of games and picked up a second League Championship medal in 1969-70.

After playing in 399 League and Cup games for Everton, Gordon West left the Goodison club at the end of the 1972-73 season, having won three England caps - there might have been more but for his withdrawl for family reasons.

He was lured back to the game two years after making his last appearance for Everton by neighbours Tranmere Rovers. Meanwhile, Everton were not to find a truly satisfactory replacement him until the arrival of Neville Southall.

Young failed to control a bouncing ball and Derek Temple carried on running, drawing Springett from his goal before scoring Everton's third goal and so complete one of the club's most famous victories.

During the summer, Ray Wilson was a member of the England team that won the World Cup. Another star of that England team was Blackpool's Alan Ball, who, a few weeks after the final, joined Everton for a club record fee of £110,000.

With Liverpool winning the League Championship, the Charity Shield was played at Goodison but the Blues went down 1-0.

The 1966-67 season saw a number of changes in personnel around Goodison as both youngsters and newcomers were given their chance.

TOMMY WRIGHT

A former England Schoolboy international, full-back Tommy Wright joined Everton as an inside-forward before being converted to wing-half and finally the position where he made his name. He made his first team debut for the Toffees in a 1-1 draw at Blackpool in October 1964 as a replacement for Scottish international Alex Parker.

Wright was a virtual ever-present in the Everton side for the next nine seasons, winning an FA Cup winners' medal in 1966 as the Blues beat Sheffield Wednesday 3-2.

In 1968 he won the first of 11 full caps for England when he played against Russia in the European Championships third place play-off. He also represented his country in the 1970 World Cup Finals in Mexico.

Tommy Wright was one of the most constructive back-four players in the Football League and liked nothing better than to force his way down the flanks when the opportunity arose.

When Everton won the League Championship in 1969-70, Wright was one of four ever-presents. Though he only scored four goals for the Blues, the one he scored against Nottingham Forest in November 1969 proved to be the only one of the game and gave Everton two vital points in their quest for the Championship.

One of football's natural gentlemen, Tommy Wright went on to play in 371 League and Cup games for Everton before hanging up his boots.

Alex Scott moved back north to Hibernian and long-serving Brian Harris decided to join Cardiff City. Derek Temple joined Preston North End and Dennis Stevens, who lost his place to Colin Harvey, moved on to Oldham Athletic. Scottish international Jimmy Gabriel signed for Southampton whilst the popular Fred Pickering was transferred to Birmingham City. Among the youngsters to replace them were Jimmy Husband, John Hurst, Howard Kendall, Joe Royle and Tommy Wright.

After an indifferent start to the season, Everton embarked on an 11-match unbeaten run which included an exciting 5-4 home win over West Bromwich Albion. A Johnny Morrissey hat-trick in a 4-1 defeat of Sunderland on the final day of the season gave the Blues a finishing posi-

SANDY BROWN

Following their League Championship success in 1962-63, Everton went north of the border and paid Partick Thistle £38,000 for the services of Alex 'Sandy' Brown. He proved to be one of Everton's most versatile players. The wearer of eight different numbered outfield shirts, Brown could also play in goal and it was this versatility that led to him being named substitute in no fewer than 43 League and Cup games.

Brown made his Everton debut in a 4-3 home defeat at the hands of Burnley and over the next seven seasons was a valued member of the Toffees' squad.

When Everton enteratined Leeds United in the mid-1960s, Brown was sent-off in the opening minutes of a match in which the referee later had to lead both teams off the field for a cooling-down period. Though he played in four of the club's FA Cup ties in 1966, he wasn't selected for the final itself. In 1969-70 he appeared in 36 games as the Blues won the League Championship. Brown had scored 11 goals in 251 League and Cup games when he left Goodison in 1971 to join Shrewsbury Town.

After a short stay at Gay Meadow, he signed for Southport and in 1972-73 was an important member of the Sandgrounders Fourth Division Championship-winning side. At the end of that season he left to play non-League football for Northern Premier League club Fleetwood.

COLIN HARVEY

Colin Harvey made his Everton debut in a European Cup tie at Inter Milan's San Siro Stadium but smoke bombs and fireworks along with the baying of over 90,000 Italians did not intimidate the 18-year-old. He played with great maturity as the Blues lost by a single goal to one of the best club sides in the world.

He established himself in the Everton side the following season, when he played in his first Merseyside derby. Everton won 4-0 and Harvey got on the scoresheet. However, he wasn't a prolific scorer and even his best-remembered goal, the winner at Burnden Park in the 1966 FA Cup semi-final against Manchester United was mis-hit, bobbling over Harry Gregg from 15 yards!

Surprisingly, Harvey, who had every attribute demanded of a modern midfield player, only won one England cap and that was in 1971 when Malta were beaten 1-0. He had played in 384 games for the Blues when in October 1974 he moved to Sheffield Wednesday for £70,000. Sadly a nagging hip injury caught up with him and just over a year after arriving at Hillsborough he was forced to retire.

He took up coaching and turned out to be a natural. There is no doubt that he can take much of the credit for Everton's success in the mid 1980s, but he was not cut out to be a manager. When he succeeded Howard Kendall in the summer of 1987 he seemed almost reluctant to do so, knowing deep down that it was not the right role for him. He was dismissed at the end of October 1990 but six days later he returned to Goodison as assistant-manager following the appointment of Howard Kendall. He later left Goodison to become assistant-manager to Graeme Sharp at Oldham Athletic before both former Blues resigned their posts in February 1997.

tion of sixth - quite a commendable achievement considering the youth and inexperience in the team.

In the FA Cup, the Blues beat Burnley and Wolves, both matches necessitating replays, before taking on Liverpool in round five. A crowd of 64,851 crammed into Goodison to see Alan Ball score the game's only goal and so set up a quarter-final tie at Nottingham Forest. Sadly, two goals from Jimmy Husband were not enough and Forest won 3-2.

Having won the FA Cup, Everton played in the European Cup

Winners' Cup. After beating Aalborg 2-1 on aggregate, the Blues lost by the same scoreline in round two to tough Spanish side Real Zaragoza.

The 1967-68 season brought a marginal improvement in the club's league form as they finished one place higher in fifth position. Alan Ball was the Blues' leading scorer, his total of 20 goals in 34 league games included four in a 6-2 win at West Bromwich Albion. He was well supported by Joe Royle, who found the net 16 times in 33 league outings. Royle had made his Everton debut at Blackpool in January 1966 at the age of 16 years 288 days to become the youngest-ever player to represent the club.

In the FA Cup, Royle scored his first-ever goal in the competition as the Blues won 1-0 at Southport in round three. The fourth round brought another away tie, this time at Carlisle United, but goals from Husband and Royle were enough to defeat the Second Division outfit. Tranmere Rovers were the visitors for a fifth round tie that attracted 61,982 spectators to Goodison and though the side from the Wirral put up a strong fight, they went down 2-0. That result took the Blues into the sixth round where a comfortable 3-1 win at Leicester City put them into their fourteenth FA Cup semi-final. Their opponents at Old Trafford were Leeds United but despite missing Ball and Hurst, Everton surprised the Yorkshire club with Johnny Morrissey scoring the game's only goal. Everton were through to their seventh FA Cup Final and their second in three years.

FA Cup Final 1968: Everton 0 West Bromwich Albion 1

Everton were clear favourites to win the FA Cup, their 6-2 thrashing of the Baggies at the Hawthorns being only eight weeks ago. However, Albion had performed well in the last few weeks of the campaign and had finished eighth, just six points behind Everton. In one of the dreariest finals for years, both defences were on top and at the end of ninety minutes the game was goalless, although Jimmy Husband missed an easy chance to win the game for the Blues in the dying minutes. The game was settled in extra-time when Albion's England centre-forward Jeff Astle's shot was blocked by West before he managed to hit the rebound with his other foot into the top corner of the net. It was a superb goal and the only moment of real note throughout the entire 120 minutes!

Harry Catterick's team now seemed capable of challenging for every

HOWARD KENDALL

Howard Kendall was the youngest player ever to appear in an FA Cup Final when he played left-half for Preston North End against West Ham United in 1964 just twenty days before his 18th birthday. After making 104 appearances for North End, Kendall joined Everton for £80,000 in March 1967. Two days after putting pen to paper he made his debut for the Toffees against Southampton.

A former England Youth captain, he went on to be part of one of the most influential midfield combinations that Everton have ever had. Along with Ball and Harvey he helped the Blues to an emphatic League Championship success in 1969-70 and was unlucky not to win full international honours. After playing in 274 League and Cup games, in which he scored 29 goals, he left Goodison to join Birmingham City in February 1974 as part of a complicated £350,000 deal which brought Bob Latchford to Everton. In August 1977 he joined Stoke City where he became the club's coach under Alan Durban. He then became player-manager of Blackburn Rovers and, having taken the Ewood Park club from the Third Division to the brink of top flight football, he was ready for the big-time.

In May 1981, Kendall returned to the scene of his greatest triumphs. Though he led the club to eighth place in his first season in charge he struggled to come to terms with the job. Despite a significant improvement in Everton's fortunes, the Goodison trophy cabinet was still bare but in 1983-84 the club won the FA Cup and reached the final of the League Cup. The following season Everton won the League Championship and the European Cup Winners' Cup as well as reaching the FA Cup Final. Not surprisingly, Kendall was named Manager of the Year. After winning the League Championship again in 1986-87 Kendall left to manage Atletico Bilbao. He has since managed Manchester City, Everton again, Notts County, Sheffield United and Everton for a third time, parting company with the club following a season in which they hung on to their Premiership status on goal difference from Bolton Wanderers.

honour in the game and in 1968-9 they battled vigorously in their quest for the Championship. After two defeats in the opening three games, Everton embarked on an unbeaten run of 16 games, including a 4-0 win

over last season's FA Cup Final opponents West Bromwich Albion, a match in which Alan Ball netted a hat-trick. The Blues' unbeaten run came to an end at Leeds United as the eventual champions won 2-1. Everton bounced back in the next game, beating Leicester City 7-1 with top-scorer Joe Royle netting a hat-trick, but had to settle for third place behind Leeds and Liverpool..

The Blues had returned to League Cup action the previous season but after two big wins over Tranmere Rovers (Home 4-0) and Luton Town (Home 5-1) they lost 1-0 at Derby County after the first meeting at Goodison had ended goalless. The FA Cup brought another good run as Joe Royle scored in every round to set up a semi-final meeting with Manchester City at Villa Park. Despite having a lot of the game, Everton went down 1-0 to Joe Mercer's side who went on to take the Cup.

Everton won their first four games of the 1969-70 season, conceding just one goal in the process. In fact, the Blues were undefeated in the opening seven games and lost just one of the first 18 matches. Joe Royle netted a hat-trick in a 4-2 defeat of Southampton whilst the club's best win was a 6-2 thrashing of Stoke City. Driven on by the midfield trio of Harvey, Kendall and Ball, the Blues sat proudly on top of the table and save for a handful of weeks when they occupied second place behind Leeds United, they were still on top of the League when the season ended in April. It was a superb campaign at the end of which they headed the Elland Road club by nine points having lost only five games. The Blues had won the title with style and gained countless admirers. Joe Royle was the club's leading scorer with 23 goals whilst the man Harry Catterick described as 'the greatest Everton discovery of all time', Alan Whittle struck 11 goals in just 15 games.

It was Everton's seventh Championship and had been won with a

JOE ROYLE

Joe Royle became the youngest-ever player to wear the famous royal blue when on 15 January 1966, at the age of 16 years 288 days, he played at Blackpool. He had been called in to replace the axed Alex Young but when furious fans attacked manager Harry Catterick, Royle returned to the club's Central League side. He worked hard to improve his game and by the start of the 1967-68 season he won and fully deserved a regular first team spot.

In 1968-69, Royle was the Blues leading scorer with 22 goals including a hat-trick in a 7-1 home win over Leicester City. He top-scored for Everton for the next three seasons, scoring a hat-trick against Southampton in September 1969 (Home 4-2) and then four goals against the same opposition in November 1971 as the Saints were beaten 8-0. He was capped ten times at Under-23 level and made his bow for the full England team against Malta in February 1971. He had scored 119 goals in 275 League and Cup games when he was transferred to Manchester City for £200,000 in December 1974.

He scored 31 goals in 117 games for the Maine Road club before moving to Bristol City for £90,000 in November 1977. After three years at Ashton Gate he joined Norwich City, where his playing career came to a premature end because of injury.

Entering management with Oldham Athletic he combined integrity, humour and sound judgement as the Latics won promotion from the Second Division and reached the League Cup Final and FA Cup semi-final.

In November 1994 he returned to Goodison as manager and, though he kept the club in the Premiership, there were clashes with chairman Peter Johnson over transfer deals and these resulted in Royle quitting the club by mutual consent.

Royle is now manager of Manchester City, having taken the Maine Road club into the Premiership after successive promotions.

club record 66 points, ten more than Dixie Dean's famous side of 1931-32.

The final placings were as follows:

	P.	W.	D.	L.	F.	A.	Pts
Everton	42	29	8	5	72	34	66
Leeds United	42	21	15	6	84	49	57
Chelsea	42	21	13	8	70	50	55

After their Championship-winning season, the Blues made a disastrous start to the 1970-71 campaign. They failed to win any of their opening six games but then won four matches in succession! They finished a disappointing 14th in the League and only Joe Royle, with 17 goals, managed to get into double figures.

There was some compensation in the FA Cup with the Blues reaching the semi-final before losing to Liverpool. Two goals from Jimmy Husband gave Everton a 2-0 home win over Blackburn Rovers in round three before Middlesbrough were beaten 3-0 in the fourth round. That victory set up a fifth round meeting with Derby County, where only a David Johnson goal separated the sides. In the quarter-finals, Everton were drawn at home for the fourth time, their opponents Fourth Division Colchester United. Though they had defeated Leeds United in the previous round, they were no match for Everton, who won 5-0. The semi-final against Liverpool was played at Old Trafford but before the game got underway, manager Harry Catterick was taken ill and the side left in the charge of coach Will Dixon. The Blues were on top but after Brian Labone was forced to limp off the park with a pulled hamstring, they lost their composure and went down 2-1.

The League Championship triumph had brought European Cup football back to Goodison Park and in the first round first leg Alan Ball netted a hat-trick in a 6-2 home win over Icelandic champions Keflavik. They netted a further three goals in the away leg to qualify for round two, where they met much tougher opposition in German champions, Borussia Monchengladbach. Howard Kendall netted a vital away goal in a 1-1 draw in Germany before the teams lined-up two weeks later on a rainy night at Goodison. The Blues took the lead after only 24 seconds when Johnny Morrissey's shot cum cross was fumbled over the line by the German 'keeper. It was then Andy Rankin's turn, failing to hold a long-range shot and allowing Laumen to tap home for the equaliser.

ALAN BALL

One of the greatest players ever to pull on the royal blue shirt of Everton, Alan Ball was never out of the spotlight. After unsuccessful trials with Wolves and Bolton it was only the persistence of his footballing father, Alan Ball senior, that persuaded Blackpool to sign him. He made his first team debut for the Seasiders against Liverpool at Anfield in 1962 at 17 years of age. Within twelve months he had become a regular in the Bloomfield Road club's side and went on to play in 126 games for them before joining Everton in August 1966  immediately after his scintillating performances for England in their World Cup victory. The £110,000 fee was then the highest to pass between British clubs. Ball made his Everton debut at Fulham on the opening day of the 1966-67 season, scoring the game's only goal.

He was the club's leading scorer in his first two seasons with the Toffees and in 1967-68, when he scored 20 league goals, netted four in the 6-2 win at West Bromwich Albion. Playing alongside Colin Harvey and Howard Kendall in the Everton midfield, he was instrumental in the Blues winning the League Championship in 1969-70. For no apparent reason the side broke up and in 1971, after scoring 78 goals in 249 games, Ball was sold to Arsenal for another record fee of £220,000.

After a successful career at Arsenal, Ball moved to Southampton for £60,000 in March 1976, then to Blackpool as manager in 1980. He resigned a year later and returned to Southampton, playing his last game in the top flight in October 1982. After a short spell in Hong Kong he resumed his playing career with Bristol Rovers before managing Portsmouth. After taking Pompey into the First Division he had spells managing Stoke City, Exeter City, Southampton and Manchester City before returning to Fratton Park for a second spell as Portsmouth boss.

JOHN HURST

John Hurst arrived at Goodison Park in a blaze of publicity in May 1962. The 14-year-old England Schoolboy international was converted from centre-forward to defensive wing-half and after a series of outstanding displays in the club's successful FA Youth Cup campaign of 1965, he made his league debut as a substitute in a 1-1 draw at Stoke City in August 1965.

One of the finest uncapped wing-halves in the country, Hurst was comfortable in possession and an intelligent reader of the game, being far more likely to make a perceptive interception than be forced into a desperate challenge. In 1968, Hurst confounded medical experts who said he would neevr play again that season after contracting hepatitis on the eve of the FA Cup semi-final against Leeds United. Against all odds, he recovered in time to play in the final against West Bromwich Albion.

Hurst was an ever-present for the next two seasons, including the League Championship-winning campaign of 1969-70. He went on to score 34 goals in 399 League and Cup games before being allowed to leave Goodison Park in the summer of 1976 and join Oldham Athletic.

One of the game's most polished players, Hurst spent five enjoyable and effective seasons at Boundary Park appearing in 170 games before retiring in 1981.

The quietest man in the Everton dressing-room, 'Gentleman Jack', as he was known, was a most respected and impeccable professional who always let his football do the talking.

Though both sides had chances to take the lead, there was no further scoring and the game went to a penalty shoot-out. With the score at 4-3 in Everton's favour, Rankin flung himself full length to save Muller's penalty and take the Blues through to a third round meeting with Panathinaikos of Greece. Though David Johnson opened the scoring in the first leg at Goodison, the Greek side scored a vital equaliser and with the second leg in Athens goalless, Panathinaikos went through on the away goals rule.

In 1971-72 Everton failed to score in 19 league games, though on 20 November 1971 they beat Southampton 8-0 with Joe Royle scoring four times and David Johnson netting a hat-trick. Those two players were the Blues' joint-top scorers with nine goals apiece! Manager Harry Catterick had written in the FA Cup semi-final programme against Liverpool that he would expect a transfer fee of a million pounds for Alan Ball. 'We would consider it,' he added, 'and then we would say "no".' So it came as a great shock in December 1971 when the inspiration behind Everton's recent triumphs was sold to Arsenal for a record fee of £220,000! Five days into the New Year, manager Harry Catterick suffered a heart attack and though he was back at work within three months, it marked the beginning of the end of his reign as Goodison boss. Everton ended the season in 15th place but worse was to come in 1972-73 when, despite being undefeated in their opening eight games, the Blues sank even lower to finish 17th.

The club's performances in the Cup competitions had also been disappointing and so the Everton board decided it was time for a change at the top and so, at the end of the season, Catterick stepped aside, moving into a consultancy position with the club.

His replacement was former Everton winger Billy Bingham, who had enjoyed three successful seasons at Goodison in the early 1960s. He soon entered the transfer market, paying Birmingham City £350,000 for the services of Bob Latchford, making him the most expensive player in Britain. Though the Blues were never in contention for the title, Bingham took the club to seventh spot in the First Division - an encouraging start.

In 1974-75, Everton lost just one of their first 21 games as they made a serious challenge for the title. However, in that opening spell, the Blues drew eight of nine successive games. At the turn of the year, Everton were top of the table and though results in the second half of the campaign were mixed, they were still clinging on to top spot with just four games still to play.

Sadly, they lost two and drew one of those games and ended the season in fourth place just three points behind the champions, Derby County.

Hopes were high at the start of the 1975-76 season but Bingham's squad was racked by injuries and with the Irishman still experimenting, he was forced to use 27 players during the campaign. Goals were the main stumbling block with only Bob Latchford reaching double figures. Everton finished the season in 11th place, well behind rivals Liverpool, who captured the title for the first time under new manager Bob Paisley.

In that season's UEFA Cup competition, the Blues had the misfortune to be drawn against top Italian club AC Milan. The first leg at Goodison was goalless and, though Everton defended resolutely in Italy, Milan won by a single goal.

Everton began the 1976-77 campaign in fine style with Bob Latchford scoring twice on the opening day of the season in a 4-0 win at Queen's Park Rangers. However, as the pitches grew muddy, the Blues began to slide and Bingham was forced to enter the transfer market. He paid Belgian club Anderlecht £200,000 for the services of the mercurial striker Duncan McKenzie and a similar amount for Derby County's Scottish international midfielder Bruce Rioch. Sadly, the new signings did little to arrest the slide and in January 1977, Bingham was sacked. He was replaced by Gordon Lee, who arrived at Goodison a week after Bingham's departure. Though the Blues were in 18th place in the First Division they had just qualified for the semi-finals of the League Cup where their opponents were Second Division Bolton Wanderers. In the first leg at Goodison, the visitors were the better team and fully deserved their last minute equaliser in a 1-1 draw. A crowd of 50,413 crammed into Burnden Park for the second leg, Bolton's biggest crowd for years. Bob Latchford scored the only goal of the game to send Everton through to the Wembley final against Aston Villa.

League Cup Final 1977: Everton 0 Aston Villa 0

Aston Villa had already won the trophy twice and were confident of

JIMMY HUSBAND

Unorthodox winger Jimmy Husband was a likebale and talented player. Born in Newcastle, he played his early football with local club Shields before a series of impressive performances led to Everton securing his services in the summer of 1963.

Nicknamed 'Skippy' by Everton fans because of his distinctive running style, Husband made his Blues' debut in a 1-1 draw at Fulham in April 1965. The following season he made his European debut as a 17-year-old in the 2-1 second round second leg win over Ujpest Dozsa.

In 1968-69, Husband had his best season in terms of goals scored, netting 20 in 43 League and Cup games. The following campaign he was a regular member of Everton's League Championship-winning side scoring some vital goals, perhaps none more so than both goals in the 2-1 win against his home-town team, Newcastle United.

Husband won England Under-23 honours and was on the verge of the full international side a number of times but was never selected.

In November 1973 after scoring 55 goals in 197 League and Cup games, Husband was allowed to leave Everton and join Luton Town.

He spent five seasons at Kenilworth Road, scoring 44 goals in 143 league games for the Hatters before hanging up his boots.

In 1984 he was tempted out of retirement to play for a Bedfordshire village side - their name, Everton!

winning it a third time. Sadly, the final was a dire affair with goalscoring opportunities few and far between. Everton's best chance came early in the game when Duncan McKenzie completely wrong-footed the entire Villa defence to set up a scoring opportunity for Latchford that was wasted. Not surprisingly, the game ended goalless even after extra-time.

League Cup Final(Replay) 1977: Everton 1 Aston Villa 1

The two teams met again at Hillsborough a few days later with the injured Martin Dobson and David Jones being replaced by Roger Kenyon and Mike Bernard. Kenyon, whose progress had been hampered by a car accident in 1974, had the misfortune to put through his own goal to give Villa the lead. Despite a lot of pressure, the Blues were still searching for the equaliser as the game entered the final minute. Then,

ROGER KENYON

Seen as the natural replacement for long-serving centre-half Brian Labone, Roger Kenyon was a reliable and consistent defender. He made his Everton debut in a 2-2 draw at Arsenal in November 1967 and went on to play his early games for the club alongside the Everton captain.

He was substitute but did not play in Everton's FA Cup Final side of 1968 and only made nine appearances in Everton's League Championship-winning side of 1969-70. Towards the end of that campaign, his performances in the heart of the Everton defence earned him some glowing tributes and from then on he became the club's first-choice pivot.

The team's performances went into decline and Kenyon's career wasn't helped when he was badly injured in a car crash in 1974. Despite being dogged by a series of niggling injuries, Kenyon was an England substitute for the European Championship games against West Germany, Cyprus and Wales at Wembley the following year.

Kenyon remained at Goodison Park until midway through the 1978-79 season when, after scoring nine goals in 306 League and Cup games, he left the club, moving to the west coast of Canada to play for Vancouver Whitecaps.

In his first season he helped steer them to the North American Soccer League title.

with all looking to be lost, up popped Bob Latchford to slam home Kenyon's deep cross and take the tie into extra-time. There were no further goals and yet again the two teams were forced to replay.

League Cup Final (2nd Replay) 1977: Everton 2 Aston Villa 3

The venue for the third meeting was Old Trafford. Everton went ahead through Bob Latchford but Chris Nicholl soon equalised for Villa, who took the lead a minute later when Brian Little fired home from close range. Everton continued to battle hard and fully deserved their equaliser when Mick Lyons beat Villa 'keeper John Burridge after Martin Dobson had headed against the bar. For the third time the game went into extra-time but with another replay looking certain, Villa ended the long-drawn out affair when Brian Little netted his second and Villa's third goal to win the trophy for the Midlands side.

Ten days after this game, the Blues were back in Mnchester, this time at Maine Road for the FA Cup semi-final against Liverpool. To reach this stage of the competition, Everton had beaten Stoke City (Home 2-0), Swindon Town (Home 2-1 after a 2-2 draw), Cardiff City (Away 2-1) and Derby County (Home 2-0).

For the semi-final clash, both Everton and Liverpool had been hit by injuries with Latchford, Kenyon and Jones all missing for the Blues. Liverpool supersub David Fairclough, playing from the start due to the injury crisis, should have scored in the first minute but the Reds did take the lead through Terry McDermott. Everton soon got back into the game and equalised just before half-time through Duncan McKenzie. A mistake by Everton 'keeper David Lawson gifted Jimmy Case a goal but he soon made amends, saving well from former team-mate David Johnson. Everton weren't finished and Bruce Rioch equalised. There were just minutes remaining when Bryan Hamilton hit what looked to be the winner but referee Clive Thomas ruled him offside and a replay was necessary.

Referee Thomas once again played a hand with the first goal in the replay four days later, awarding Liverpool a penalty after Pejic was adjudged to have pushed Johnson. After Neal had smashed home the spot-kick, Case and Kennedy added further goals to clinch Liverpool's place at Wembley.

After playing in 58 games that season, it was little wonder that the

MICK LYONS

Mick Lyons joined Everton as a striker and played in the forward line for both the Youth and Central League sides, but when David Johnson emerged from the shadows, Tommy Casey decided to switch Lyons to centre-back. Lyons made his league debut for the Toffees in a 3-2 defeat at Nottingham Forest in March 1971, going on to build an outstanding career for himself.

By the mid-1970s, Lyons had won his spurs, fully deserving the England Under-23 caps, 'B' international recognition and club captaincy that came his way.

Throughout his twelve years at Goodison Park, Lyons never once finished on the winning side in a Merseyside derby, missing the only two Everton victories. He was 'Mr Everton' to many supporters, a player who would readily run through a brick wall to further the Everton cause, but lost his first team place in 1982. After scoring 59 goals in 460 games, he severed his connection with the club and joined Sheffield Wednesday.

He helped the Owls to win promotion to the First Division before becoming player-coach at Grimsby Town. However, after the Mariners were relegated to the Third Division in 1986-87 he was sacked.

A month later he rejoined Everton as coach under Colin Harvey before taking similar jobs, first with Wigan Athl;etic and then Huddersfield Town. He later accepted a post of coach to the Brunei national team.

Blues stumbled at the final hurdle. However, with a final league placing of ninth, a League Cup Final contested three times and a twice-fought FA Cup semi-final, Gordon Lee could look back on his first few months in office with some satisfaction.

During the close season there was a flurry of transfer activity with Queen's Park Rangers winger Dave Thomas and Blackpool's Scottish international goalkeeper George Wood arriving at Goodison. There was also something of a clear-out with Bryan Hamilton, Ken McNaught and Bruce Rioch all parting company with the club.

The 1977-78 season began with Everton losing their opening two games, the first 3-1 at home to newly promoted Nottingham Forest. After losing 1-0 at Arsenal three days later, the Blues embarked on an

18-match unbeaten run which took the club into second place in the First Division. During that sequence, Bob Latchford scored four times in a 5-1 win at Queen's Park Rangers and netted a hat-trick in a 6-0 defeat of Coventry City. Everton's next defeat was at home to Manchester United on Boxing Day when Dave Sexton's team won 6-2. They recovered from that defeat and although they were always in contention for the title, they could never close the gap on Nottingham Forest, who finished nine points ahead of the Blues.

Bob Latchford, who was at last proving to be an effective goalscorer, reached the final game of the season at home to Chelsea, needing two

BOB LATCHFORD

Bob Latchford made his name with his home-town team, Birmingham City, scoring 84 goals in 194 games. He signed for Everton in February 1974 for a fee of £350,000 and made his debut in a 4-3 defeat at West Ham United.

In his first four full seasons with the Toffees, Latchford was the top league goalscorer, reaching his peak in 1977-78 when he became the first Division One player for six years to reach the 30-goal mark. Latchford's total included four in a 5-1 win at Queen's Park Rangers. He reached the final game of that season at home to Chelsea needing two goals to claim a national newspaper prize of £10,000. Everton won 6-0 and Latchford netted the goals necessary to win the money and carve a place for himself in Merseyside football folklore.

Whilst at Goodison, Latchford won 12 full international caps for England, the first against Italy in 1977. In the summer of 1981, after scoring 138 goals in 289 League and Cup games, he left to join Swansea City for £125,000.

He enjoyed mixed fortunes in South Wales but he did score 32 goals in 1982-83 before being given a free transfer and joining Dutch club Breda.

Within five months he had returned to England and signed for Coventry City. Twelve months later, he left to play for Lincoln City, ending his league career with Newport County.

goals to claim a national newspaper prize of £10,000. Everton won 6-0 and Latchford netted the goals necessary to win the money and carve a place for himself in Merseyside football folklore.

Everton made their best-ever start to a Football League season in 1978-79 when they were unbeaten for the first 19 games before losing 3-2 at Coventry City. However goals were hard to come by and towards the end of the season, Brian Kidd arrived from Manchester City for a fee of £120,000. Another addition to the squad was Derby County's England international defender Colin Todd but sadly he clashed with Lee and within a year he was on his way out of Goodison. Everton, who at one time topped the First Division table, had to settle for fourth place, 17 points behind League Champions, Liverpool.

Back in Europe after a three-year gap, the Blues drew Irish club Finn Harps in the first round of the UEFA Cup. They won both legs 5-0 but in the next round faced much tougher competition in Czech side Dukla Prague. Goals from King and Latchford gave Everton a 2-1 win in the home leg but the Blues lost 1-0 in the Czech capital to go out on the away goals rule.

During the course of the club's centenary year of 1979-80, Lee added further players to the Everton squad in a bid to bring the glory days back to Goodison. In came Peter Eastoe, Gary Stanley, Asa Hartford, John

MARTIN DOBSON

Martin Dobson began his career as a centre-forward with Bolton Wanderers but he was eventually handed a free transfer. He considered giving up the game but his father persuaded Burnley manager Harry Potts to give him a trial at Turf Moor. On joining the Clarets, Dobson was switched from front-runner to midfield where he won international recognition, being called up for the England Under-23s against Bulgaria at Plymouth. In 1972-73 he captained Burnley to the Second Division Championship and the following season led them to sixth place in the First Division and to the FA Cup semi-finals. Four days after the semi-final he won the first of five full caps for England when he played against Portugal.

In August 1974, Dobson moved to Everton for £300,000, a new British transfer record. He made his debut for the Toffees in a 2-1 home win over Arsenal and in five years with the club was virtually an ever-present. He figured in two UEFA Cup campaigns and in 1977 played in the FA Cup semi-final defeat by Liverpool and the three-game marathon League Cup Final against Aston Villa.

In the 1978-79 League Cup campaign he scored a hat-trick when Everton achieved their best-ever scoreline, beating Wimbledon 8-0.

It was perhaps a surprise when Dobson returned to Turf Moor in the summer of 1979 after scoring 40 goals in 230 games.

He captained Burnley to the Third Division Championship in 1982-83 before moving to Bury where he later became their player-manager. After a spell as manager of Bristol Rovers he is now Youth Development Officer with his first club, Bolton Wanderers.

Gidman and Gary Megson, but buying so many players was not the solution to Everton's problems as results quickly demonstrated. It was a disastrous season, ending with the Blues in 19th place just five points away from relegation.

However, the Blues had a fine run in the FA Cup and, after beating Aldershot (Home 4-1), Wigan Athletic (Home 3-0), Wrexham (Home 5-2) and Ipswich Town (Home 2-1), met West Ham United in the semifinal at Villa Park. The game ended all-square at 1-1 with the Hammers winning the Elland Road replay 2-1. In the UEFA Cup, Everton again made an early exit, beaten 1-0 home and away by the former European champions, Feyenoord of Holland.

The 1980-81 season was just as bad and, although they won six consecutive matches in September and October to go into third place, by the end of the season they had plummeted to 15th position. The Goodison faithful were now displaying open hostility towards Gordon Lee and his players and two days after the season had finished, the Everton manager was dismissed.

Everton's new manager was former Goodison favourtite Howard Kendall. He had been in charge of Blackburn Rovers for a couple of seasons, taking them from the Third Division to within three points of promotion to the top flight. When he arrived on Merseyside, Everton were firmly in the shadow of Liverpool with Blues' supporters demanding the same sort of success. One of Kendall's first jobs was to sell Bob Latchford to Swansea City for £125,000. Though he had taken a little time to settle, Latchford had scored 138 goals in 286 games to make him Everton's most prolific scorer since the Second World War.

Though Everton beat Birmingham City 3-1 on the opening day of the 1981-82 season, results over the first half of the campaign were mixed. By the turn of the year, Everton were in mid-table but out of both the FA and League Cup competitions. Kendall made a couple of signings during the course of the season that were to stand him in good stead over the next few seasons. Neville Southall cost £150,000 from Bury, whilst Adrian Heath arrived for £800,000 from Stoke City, making him Everton's record signing. The Blues ended the season with five wins and a draw out of their last six matches to end the season in eighth place.

During the close season, Kendall crossed Stanley Park to sign two

Liverpool players in former Everton striker David Johnson and Kevin Sheedy.

Though it seemed that Everton now had the nucleus of a League Championship-winning team, they soon found themselves at the wrong end of the table. Following a humiliating 5-0 defeat at home to Liverpool, the Blues made a number of defensive changes, bringing in Jim Arnold in goal and Gary Stevens for Brian Borrows at right-back. The club made another important signing just before the turn of the year when Peter Reid arrived from Bolton Wanderers for £60,000. In the second half of the season, the Blues looked a completely different team and with Sheedy and Sharp scoring 26 goals between them, Everton ended the campaign in seventh place.

In that season's FA Cup, Everton had beaten Newport County and Shrewsbury Town before facing cup holders Tottenham Hotspur in round five. Though the North London club were most people's favourites to retain the trophy, goals from King and Sharp put the Blues into the quarter-finals where their opponents were Manchester United. Unfortunately, despite having a lot of the game, Everton lost 1-0.

There was only one acquisition during the summer of 1983 when Trevor Steven arrived from Burnley for a fee of £300,000.

Though there was considerable optimism before the start of the 1983-84 season, this was soon dispelled following five defeats in the opening twelve games, the last a 3-0 reversal at Liverpool. There was a definite shortage of goals, a problem Kendall hoped to solve by signing Scottish international centre-forward Andy Gray from Wolverhampton Wanderers. However, it took him a while to settle and at the end of the year, the Blues, who had scored just 11 goals in 21 games, lay in sixteenth place. Gates had slumped to around the 20,000 mark and in the League Cup tie against Chesterfield just 8,000 turned up to see the 2-2 draw. Fortunately the Blues had won the first leg at Saltergate 1-0 to go through to round three. After victories over Coventry City and West Ham United, Everton met Oxford United at the Manor Ground in the fifth round. The Blues went a goal down early in the second-half, then with just ten minutes to play, Oxford defender Kevin Brock attempted a risky backpass to his goalkeeper and Adrian Heath intercepted the ball and rounded the 'keeper to level the scores. The game ended in a 1-1

ANDY KING

Andy King joined the Toffees from his home-town club Luton Town in April 1976 when Everton manager Billy Bingham paid £35,000 for his services. King made his debut in a 3-1 win over Middlesbrough, and though he failed to score in that game, he did score a number of vital goals for the club throughout his Everton career.

Andy King was idolised by Everton fans who appreciated this hugely gifted player. In 1977-78, King was ever-present as the Blues finished third in Division One, his form almost bringing him full international honours. In 1978-79, King netted his only hat-trick for the club in a 4-1 home win over Bristol City, ending the campaign with a career-best 16. However, in September 1980, King was transferred to Queen's Park Rangers for £450,000, but after just one year at Loftus Road he moved to West Bromwich Albion for a similar fee.

King just could not live without Everton and in the summer of 1982 he returned to Goodison Park for a second spell. Sadly, he failed to realise his full potential and after scoring 68 goals in 247 League and Cup games in his two spells with the club, he was allowed to leave and went to play for Dutch side Cambuur.

He later returned to these shores to play for Wolverhampton Wanderers, Luton Town and Aldershot before entering management with Mansfield Town.

KEVIN RATCLIFFE

The most successful captain in the history of Everton Football Club, Kevin Ratcliffe made his Toffees' debut in a goalless draw at Old Trafford, subduing the fearsome Joe Jordan in March 1980, but spent the next two seasons in and out of the side. When he did play, most of his games were at left-back. Ratcliffe was upset by such apparent lack of recognition and by being played out of position so he went to confront new manager Howard Kendall. At one stage there was even talk of a move to Ipswich Town when Bobby Robson showed an interest, but thankfully he remained at Goodison Park.

In December 1982 his fortunes took a decisive upturn when he replaced the overweight Billy Wright alongside Mark Higgins in the heart of the Everton defence. Within twelve months he had succeeded the injury-ravaged Higgins as captain and the following March he was leading his country. In March 1984, at the age of 23, he became the youngest man since Bobby Moore some twenty years earlier to receive the FA Cup. Within the next year, he had led his team forward to pick up the FA Charity Shield, the League Championship and the European Cup Winners' Cup. Thereafter he skippered them to the runners-up spot in both the League and FA Cup in 1985-86 and to another League title in 1986-87.

Ratcliffe could read the game with instinctive shrewdness and could close down opponents instantly in moments of danger, often averting crises by clever positional play. Despite losing some of his astonishing speed, he continued to retain the style and consistency that made him one of the world's classiest defenders. After losing his place to Martin Keown, he was placed on the transfer list and in the spring of 1992, after playing in 461 League and Cup games, he joined Cardiff City, helping them win promotion to the new Second Division. After a spell mananging Chester City, Ratcliffe then took charge of Shrewsbury Town.

draw, a result which gave the Blues a new confidence. In the replay, Everton beat the Third Division side 4-1 to set up a two-legged semi-final against Aston Villa. In the first match at Goodison Park, the Blues won 2-0 with goals from Kevin Sheedy and Kevin Richardson, the latter playing with a broken wrist. A week later, Everton visited Villa Park and

though they dominated the first-half, hitting the woodwork on two occasions, they went down 1-0 to a late second-half goal. The 2-1 aggregate win took Everton through to their first Wembley final for seven years - their opponents, Liverpool!

League Cup FInal 1984:

Everton 0 Liverpool 0

Never before had the two Merseyside teams met in such a showdown and though Liverpool, who were probably the most formidable team in Europe, were clear favourites, Everton were not over-awed. The Blues should have gone ahead in the eighth minute when Adrian Heath beat Bruce Grobbelaar to the ball. Despite lying on the ground he hooked a shot towards the empty net only to see Alan Hansen appear to scramble the ball away with his hand!

Unbelievably the referee waved play on, refusing to listen to Everton's plea for a penalty. Though Liverpool had the better of the second-half, the game ended goalless although Graeme Sharp almost won the game for Everton with the last kick of normal time, but it wasn't to be. Extra-time also failed to produce a goal, Adrian Heath seeing his shot cleared off the line by Phil Neal.

League Cup Final (Replay) 1984: Everton 0 Liverpool 1

GRAEME SHARP

Graeme Sharp was a virtually unknown striker when Everton manager Gordon Lee paid Dumbarton £120,000 for his services in April 1980. Sharp made his debut as a substitute in a goalless draw at Brighton a month later but he took time to settle down at Goodison and even considered moving on.

Following the appointment of Howard Kendall, Sharp's career began to blossom. He enjoyed a series off ruitful combinations, first with Adrian Heath, then Andy Gray and finally Gary Lineker.

He was the scorer of the club's first goal in the 1984 FA Cup Final win over Watford. The following season he scored 30 goals and headed the equaliser against Bayern Munich in the 1984-85 European Cup Winners' Cup semi-final. His rise to stardom saw him win his first cap for Scotland when he played in a World Cup qualifier against Iceland.

Sharp's most spectacular strike came at Anfield in October 1984. Gary Stevens sent a long, high pass out of defence that dropped oblingly into the path of Sharp; he took it down on his left instep, wrong-footed Mark Lawrenson in the process and as the ball sat up perfectly for him, he hit a dipping 25-yard right-foot volley over the picturesque leap of Bruce Grobbelaar to give the Toffees a 1-0 win in the Merseyside derby.

In July 1991, Sharp, who had scored 150 goals in 432 games, left Everton for Oldham Athletic for £500,000.

When Joe Royle returned to Goodison Park, Sharp became the Latics' manager but resigned his post in February 1997.

The replay three days later was played at Maine Road. Again there was little between the two teams. Liverpool scored what turned out to be the game's only goal when Graeme Souness's fortuitous shot skidded past Neville Southall. Everton made great efforts to get themselves level but it wasn't to be and Liverpool held the trophy aloft for the fourth consecutive year.

In the FA Cup, Everton beat Stoke City 2-0 before needing three games to dispose of Gillingham. Victories over Shrewsbury Town (Home 3-0) and Notts County (Away 2-1) put the Blues just ninety minutes away from a second Wembley appearance. In the semi-final they faced Southampton at Highbury where Adrian Heath snatched a spectacular winner in extra-time.

FA Cup Final 1984: Everton 2 Watford 0

Everton were back at Wembley just seven weeks after their League Cup Final appearance against Liverpool, facing Watford, who in their 93-year history had never reached this stage of the competition before.

Watford had the better of the early exchanges but Southall and his defence held firm. Everton began to dominate the midfield with Reid and Heath working hard to open up the Watford defence. Everton opened the scoring just before half-time when Graeme Sharp's hard low drive hit the post and rebounded into the net. Six minutes into the second-half, the Blues scored again when Andy Gray challenged Watford 'keeper Steve Sherwood for a 50-50 ball. Sherwood landed on his back while the ball landed in the net. Despite the Watford protests, the referee allowed the goal and after an absence of 18 years, the Cup was coming home to Goodison.

Everton made a disastrous start to the 1984-85 season, being thrashed 4-1 at home by Tottenham Hostpur whilst two days later losing 2-1 at West Bromwich Albion.

Midfielder Paul Bracewell had joined the Blues in Cup Final week and he made his Everton debut in the FA Charity Shield against Liverpool at Wembley, starring in a 1-0 win. Everton's third fixture of the 1984-85 season saw Chelsea visit Goodison Park for a live televised match. Everton won 1-0, courtesy of a Kevin Richardson goal, and embarked on a sequence of six league games without defeat that moved them back among the First Division's leading group. One of those games

ADRIAN HEATH

Adrian Heath started his football career with his home-town club, Stoke City. After appearing briefly during the Potters' Second Division promotion-winning season of 1978-79, he became a fixture in the side the following campaign. His busy, energetic style brought him his first taste of international honours in April 1981 when he scored twice for

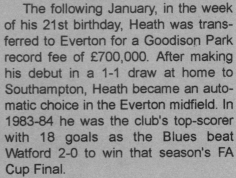

the England Under-21 side against Romania in the UEFA Championships.

The following January, in the week of his 21st birthday, Heath was transferred to Everton for a Goodison Park record fee of £700,000. After making his debut in a 1-1 draw at home to Southampton, Heath became an automatic choice in the Everton midfield. In 1983-84 he was the club's top-scorer with 18 goals as the Blues beat Watford 2-0 to win that season's FA Cup Final.

In 1984-85, when the Blues came within ninety minutes of the unprecedented treble of League, European Cup Winners' Cup and FA Cup, because of injury Heath only played a supporting role. In 1986-87 Heath won a League Championship medal playing a key role alongside Trevor Steven.

In 1988, Heath, who had scored 89 goals in 293 games, left Everton to play for Espanol of Barcelona but spent less than a season in Spain before returning for a short spell with Aston Villa. In February 1990 he joined Manchester City before later playing for Stoke City and Burnley. After the Clarets were relegated, Heath accepted the position of assistant-manager at Sheffield United before returning to Turf Moor to manage Burnley.

In the summer of 1997, Heath returned to Goodison Park as first team coach.

was against the previous season's FA Cup Final opponents Watford, the Blues winning 5-4 at Vicarage Road. After a 1-0 defeat at Arsenal, Everton won their next six games, scoring 16 goals and conceding just one - the highlight of the run being a 5-0 demolition of Manchester United. This sequence took Everton to the top of the table. Though they conceded four goals at Norwich to go down 4-2 they soon bounced back with a 5-0 win at Nottingham Forest. In their next game, the Blues conceded another four goals as Chelsea won 4-3 at Goodison, a result which knocked Everton off the top spot.

After that, Everton went an astonishing 18 matches without defeat, the best run in the club's history. Of those 18 games, no fewer than 16 were won with ten consecutive victories notched up between 23 March and 8 May that saw Everton clinch the Championship. The title was wrapped up following the Blues' 2-0 home win over Queen's Park Rangers and though they lost three of their last four matches, it hardly mattered!

The final placings at the top of Division One were:

	P.	W.	D.	L.	F.	A.	Pts
Everton	42	28	6	8	88	43	90
Liverpool	42	22	11	9	68	35	77
Tottenham Hotspur	42	23	8	11	78	51	77

In that season's European Cup Winners' Cup competition, the Blues came away from Ireland with only a goalless draw against the gallant part-timers University College, Dublin. In the second leg at Goodison Park, the Dubliners refused to lie down and were only beaten 1-0 with Graeme Sharp scoring the game's only goal. In the second round, Everton travelled to Czechoslovakia to face Slovan Bratislava. They returned with a one goal lead courtesy of a fine strike by Paul Bracewell before winning the return game 3-0. In the quarter-finals, Everton entertained Fortuna Sittard of Holland and after a goalless first-half, Andy Gray netted a hat-trick to give the Blues a comfortable lead for the journey across the North Sea. In the second leg goals from Reid and Sharp gave Everton a 5-0 aggregate win. The Blues' opponents in the semi-final were Bayern Munich, one of the strongest teams in Europe. In the first leg in the Munich Stadium, the Blues defended magnificently to force a goalless draw. In the return, the German side took the lead

NEVILLE SOUTHALL

Between leaving school and becoming a full-time footballer, Neville Southall spent six years working as a dustman, mopper-up in a cafe and a hod carrier on a building site.

While living in Llandudno he kept goal for both Bangor City and Conwy United, but it was his form for Winsford United that caused Bury to pay £6,000 for him in June 1980. In the summer of 1981, after only 44 first team appearances for the Gigg Lane club, he signed for Everton in a £150,000 deal.

Southall made his debut for the Toffees in October 1981 in a 2-1 win over Ipswich Town, but things didn't go too smoothly for him after that, and following a 5-0 defeat at home to Liverpool, he was dropped and sent on loan to Port Vale. After nine games for the Valiants he returned to Goodison Park and was an ever-present for the remainder of that and the next two seasons.

After helping Everton win the FA Cup in 1984, Southall established a peerless reputation. In 1985 he was voted the Football Writers' 'Player of the Year' and no less an authority than Pat Jennings described him as a keeper without a weakness. Southall's anticipation was superb and he was a magnificent shot-stopper, but what gave him the edge was an astonishing capacity to change direction at the last moment, sometimes even in mid-air. His part in one bizarre incident - a goalmouth sit-in after walking out of a half-time harangue by Everton manager Colin Harvey - did the big Welshman less than credit, even though Southall is his own man and was acting out of frustration rather than malice.

Southall appeared 92 times for Wales and holds Everton's club record for league appearances with 578.

After a spell on loan with Stoke City, he joined the Potters on a permanent basis before playing for Torquay United. In the 1999/2000 season he even made an appearnce for Bradford City in the Premier League.

GARY STEVENS

After joining Everton straight from school, full-back Gary Stevens made such an impression in the club's Central League side that he was given his first team debut in a 1-1 draw at West Ham United in October 1981. However, it was only following Brian Borrows' move to Bolton Wanderers twelve months later that Stevens won a regular place in the Toffees' side.

His great composure on the ball, allied to his natural sprinting ability, led to him winning full international honours for England when he played in the World Cup qualifier against Northern Ireland in February 1985. Stevens was a member of the England team which reached the 1986 World Cup quarter-finals, going on to appear in 46 games for his country.

For Everton he won two League Championship winners' medals, an FA Cup winners' medal and a European Cup Winners' medal. He was a virtual ever-present in the Everton side for seven seasons, scoring 12 goals in 284 games before leaving Goodison in the summer of 1988 to join Glasgow Rangers for £1.25 million.

At Ibrox he won six Scottish Premier Division Championship medals, a Scottish Cup winners' medal and three Scottish League Cup medals.

In September 1994, after appearing in 245 first team games for the Scottish giants, he returned to Merseyside to play for Tranmere Rovers. His versatility and experience proved an invaluable asset at Prenton Park where he clocked up 150 appeaarnces.

through Hoeness but three second-half goals from Gray, Sharp and Steven took the Blues through to the final against Rapid Vienna in Rotterdam.

European Cup Winners' Cup Final 1985: Everton 3 Rapid Vienna 1

A crowd of over 50,000 gathered at Feyenoord's ultra-modern stadium with many of them having travelled across the North Sea from Merseyside. Andy Gray put the ball in the back of the net early in the game but the 'goal' was disallowed for offside. Everton had been the better side in the first-half but failed to turn their superiority into goals. However, they did take the lead early in the second-half when a disastrous back pass let in Graeme Sharp, who rounded the 'keeper and crossed for Andy Gray to slam home. The Blues soon extended their lead when Kevin Sheedy's corner was drilled home by Trevor Steven. Rapid pulled a goal back in the 80th minute through Krankl but within a minute, Sheedy shot home Everton's third goal to give the club their first European trophy.

Everton's FA Cup run that season began on a frozen pitch at Elland Road where goals from Sharp and Sheedy gave the Blues a 2-0 win over Leeds United. This was followed by another 2-0 win over Doncaster Rovers in round four before the Blues were drawn at home to non-League Telford United in the next round. Though they fought bravely, the Blues scored three times in the last thirty minutes to clinch a place in the quarter-finals. Their opponents Ipswich Town forced a 2-2 draw at Portman Road before a Graeme Sharp goal in the replay put Everton into the semi-finals with Luton Town as the opposition at Villa Park. The Hatters took the lead just before half-time and though Everton were on the offensive for most of the second-half they couldn't pierce the Luton defence. Then, with just minutes remaining, Kevin Sheedy slammed home a free-kick for the equaliser. The game went to extra-time and with Luton tiring, Derek Mountfield converted a timely cross from Kevin Sheedy to put the Blues into the final against Manchester United.

FA Cup Final 1985: Everton 0 Manchester United 1

The Blues had beaten Manchester United 5-0 at Goodison Park in a league fixture and won 2-1 at Old Trafford in the League Cup. They were in fine spirits after their European triumph three days earlier but in the end, their sixty-third game of the season proved to be just one too

DEREK MOUNTFIELD

As a youngster, Derek Mountfield would stand on the Goodison terraces dreaming of emulating his favourite players by one day representing the club he supported. However, he started his career with Tranmere Rovers and it was in the summer of 1982 that he finally joined the Blues for £30,000 after making 30 appearances for the Fourth Division club.

He made his debut in a 1-0 defeat at Birmingham City in April 1983 before being given the chance to press for a regular first team spot the following season when Mark Higgins suffered the first of a number of injuries.

Within five years, Mountfield had won an FA Cup winners' medal, two League Championship winners' medals, a European Cup Winners' Cup medal and two Charity Shield medals.

Mountfield was capped by England at Under-23 and 'B' level and was unlucky not to win full international honours.

In 1984-85, Mountfield scored 14 goals from the centre-half position, including the last-minute equaliser against Ipswich Town in the FA Cup quarter-final and the semi-final extra-time winner against Luton Town.

Following the arrival of Dave Watson, Mountfield, who had scored 24 goals in 148 games, moved to Aston Villa for £450,000. He was hampered by injuries during his four years at Villa Park but nevertheless played in 120 games, scoring 17 goals, before joining Wolverhampton Wanderers. In 1994 he moved to Carlisle United and was a key member of their 1994-95 Third Division championship-winning team. He later played for Northampton Town before ending his

many.

Everton almost took the lead early in the game when Peter Reid hit a post but the match soon settled into a midfield battle. The first-half ended goalless as both defences refused to concede any space. The game sprung to life in the 87th minute when United's Kevin Moran was sent-off after a clumsy challenge on Peter Reid. It was the Irishman's second offence and the referee had little option but to give him his marching orders, the first-ever dismissal in a Cup Final.

ANDY GRAY

Andy Gray was one of the bravest strikers of his generation. The Scottish international began his career with Dundee United, scoring 44 goals in 76 games for the Tannadice club, before moving to Aston Villa for £110,000 in September 1975.

In 1976-77, when Villa finished fourth in Division One and beat Everton in the League Cup Final, Gray was the club's leading scorer with 29 goals in 48 games. He was voted PFA 'Player of the Year' and 'Young Player of the Year'. After four years at Villa Park he moved to Wolverhampton Wanderers for a British record fee of £1.5 million. Four years later he moved again, this time to Everton for £250,000.

Gray made his Toffees' debut in a 1-0 home win over Nottingham Forest and ended the season scoring the club's second goal in the 1984 FA Cup Final win over Watford. He also scored the first goal in the 1985 European Cup Winners' Cup triumph over Rapid Vienna and, at the end of the season, he was dramatically recalled into the Scotland side, eventually ending with 20 full caps to his name. Gray had scored 22 goals in 68 games for Everton when he left Goodison in July 1985 to rejoin Aston Villa for £150,000. After a loan spell at Notts County, he signed for West Bromwich Albion but retired shortly after his arrival at the Hawthorns. In the summer of 1991 he returned to Villa Park for a third time as assistant-manager to Ron Atkinson. Gray resigned in 1992 to pursue a career in television with Sky Sports.

KEVIN SHEEDY

Kevin Sheedy began his career with Hereford United before joining Liverpool for a fee of £70,000 in the summer of 1978. Despite his outstanding Central League form for the Reds he was restricted to just two first team appearances in four years at Anfield and in June 1982 he moved to Everton for £100,000.

The young Irish midfielder made his debut for the Toffees in a 2-0 defeat at Watford on the opening day of the 1982-83 season and soon went on to prove what a bargain buy he was. One of the finest left-sided midfield players that the Blues has ever had, he was a major influence on the side that won two League Championships in the mid-1980s.

Sheedy also contributed some vital goals, such as the third in the 1985 European Cup Winners' Cup Final victory over Rapid Vienna, and some spectacular ones from free-kicks that would find their way into the top corner from 30 yards and beyond.

A Republic of Ireland international, winning 45 caps for his country, Sheedy left Goodison Park in February 1992 after scoring 92 goals in 351 League and Cup games.

He had suffered with a series of niggling injuries towards the end of his Everton career but went on to play for both Newcastle United and Blackpool before deciding to hang up his boots.

With United down to ten men, Everton fancied their chances but after ninety minutes the game was still goalless. Five minutes into extra-time, Norman Whiteside, later to join Everton, let fly with an opportunist shot which beat the outstretched arms of Neville Southall for the game's only goal.

Everton had missed the League and Cup double as well as a treble, but they were League Champions and holders of the European Cup Winners' Cup.

Prior to the start of the 1985-86 season, all English clubs suffered as UEFA imposed a ban on their playing in European competitions following the Heysel Stadium disaster in which 39 spectators, mainly followers of Juventus, lost their lives. For Everton it was a major disappointment as their League Championship success would have entitled them to compete for the European Cup.

During the close season, the Everton board caused something of a sensation when they sold Andy Gray back to his former club, Aston Villa, for £150,000. In his place came Leicester City's Gary Lineker for a club record fee of £800,000. The Blues' opening match saw them travel to Filbert Street to play Lineker's old club but they were beaten 3-1. Lineker opened his account in the fourth game of the season as Everton beat Spurs 1-0 and then, five days later, netted the first of three hat-tricks as Everton beat Birmingham City 4-1. Lineker and Sharp formed a devastating partnership, helping the Blues to some big wins, notably against Sheffield Wednesday (Away 5-1) and Arsenal (Home 6-1). By the beginning of February 1986, the Blues were top of the League with Manchester United and Liverpool their main rivals. Everton seemed the likely champions as they won nine and drew one of ten fixtures and, in fact, only lost one game in 18. During that run, Lineker netted his second hat-trick in a 4-0 defeat of Manchester City. Sadly, the Blues' challenge finally came unstuck with goalless draws at Manchester United and Nottingham Forest and a 1-0 defeat at Oxford United which ultimately cost them the title. Lineker netted his third hat-trick in a 6-1 drubbing of Southampton but Liverpool won 1-0 at Chelsea to take the title. Everton, for whom Gary Lineker scored 30 goals in 41 games, had to be content with the runners-up spot.

In the FA Cup third round, full-back Gary Stevens scored the only

PETER REID

Peter Reid was a member of the Huyton Boys team that caused something of an upset when they won the English Schools Trophy in 1970. He began his career with Bolton Wanderers, making his league debut as a substitute against Orient in October 1974. He soon established himself in the Bolton side and was ever-present for the next two seasons. His cultured midfield play and intense desire to be involved at all times were features of the Wanderers' Second Division championship-winning team of 1977-78.

Injury forced him to miss the opening games of Bolton's return to the top flight but he recovered to take his place in the side. Then, on New Year's Day 1979, he collided with Everton goalkeeper George Wood on an icy Burnden Park and broke his leg. Out of the game for over twelve months, contractual problems then prevented him from playing before he was placed on a weekly contract. In September 1981 he broke his leg again in a match at Barnsley but again won his fight for fitness and in December 1982 joined Everton for just £60,000, one of the bargain buys of all-time.

He made his debut in a 3-1 win over Nottingham Forest and soon the Reid option became irresistible. In 1984-85, his most injury-free term, Everton won the League Championship and European Cup Winners' Cup and Reid was voted the players' 'Player of the Year'. In 1986 he replaced Bryan Robson in England's World Cup side and on his return to Goodison helped the Blues win their second League title in three years. On the departure of Howard Kendall in June of that year, he became Everton's player-coach.

He had scored 13 goals in 228 games when he left to join Queen's Park Rangers. He later became player-coach at Maine Road before becoming Manchester City's manager following Kendall's return to Goodison Park. Reid is now manager of Sunderland having taken the Wearsiders into the Premier League as runaway First Division champions.

goal of the game against Fourth Division Exeter City, who put up a brave fight. Howard Kendall's former club, Blackburn Rovers, provided the opposition in the fourth round but two goals from Gary Lineker helped Everton to a 3-1 win. In the fifth round, Everton travelled to White Hart Lane to take on a Tottenham Hotspur side who were struggling near the foot of the First Division. The North London club raised their game and though the Blues won 2-1, they had Neville Southall to thank for winning a place in the quarter-finals. Drawn away at Luton Town, Everton were 2-0 down but fought back bravely and goals from Adrian Heath and Graeme Sharp forced a replay. Gary Lineker's fourth FA Cup goal settled the issue, taking Everton through to their twenty-first semi-final where their opponents at Villa Park were Sheffield Wednesday. With Lineker out injured and Trevor Steven limping off with a groin strain, the Blues struggled throughout a fairly even first-half. Substitute Alan Harper fired them ahead four minutes after the restart but the Owls equalised in the 52nd minute. There was no further scoring in normal time but in extra-time Graeme Sharp netted the goal that took Everton into the final. Their opponents were to be Liverpool, who had beaten Southampton 2-0, and so, for the first time in history, Everton and Liverpool would face each other in the FA Cup Final.

FA Cup Final 1986: Everton 1 Liverpool 3

Liverpool, who a week earlier had pipped the Blues to the League Championship, stood on the brink of a famous double. Only Everton stood between them and a new chapter in the history books!

Everton took the lead on the half-hour mark when Gary Lineker raced away from Reds' skipper Alan Hansen and sent a low drive out of Bruce Grobbelaar's reach. The Blues dominated the rest of the first-half but couldn't add to Lineker's goal. Sharp almost extended Everton's lead early in the second-half but Grobbelaar made a magnificent save.

Liverpool equalised when Whelan, fastening on to a poor clearance, played the ball to Jan Molby, who fed Ian Rush and the Welsh international made no mistake. That goal seemed to pump new life into Liverpool and the Reds added a further two goals in the final twenty minutes to run out winners 3-1. The Blues had dominated for the first seventy minutes yet Liverpool had ended victorious to become only the third side to achieve the double since the turn of the century.

74

GARY LINEKER

Gary Lineker began his career with Leicester City, where he scored 103 goals in 216 games for the Foxes before joining Everton in June 1985 for a fee of £800,000 - a figure set by an independent tribunal.

Although he was to play for only one season with the Blues, he struck up a superb attacking partnership with Graeme Sharp and scored 30 goals in 41 league games, plus another eight in Cup competitions. His league total included hat-tricks in the wins over Birmingham City (Home 4-1), Manchester City (Home 4-0) and Southampton (Home 6-1). Despite Lineker's heroics, Everton finished runners-up to Liverpool in both the League and FA Cup. Consolation was gained, however, from the fact that he was named the PFA Footballer of the Year and won the Golden Boot award as the top scorer in the World Cup Finals with six goals. He made an important contribution to England's 1986 World Cup campaign in Mexico, a first-half Lineker hat-trick blitzing away Poland. As soon as the finals were over, he moved to Barcelona for a staggering £2.3 million.

With the Spanish side he won a Spanish Cup and European Cup Winners' Cup medal, but in June 1989 he followed Terry Venables to White Hart Lane for a fee of £1.2 million. In his first season with Spurs he scored 24 goals, which meant he headed the First Division scoring charts. In 1991 he helped Spurs win the FA Cup and in the 1992 New Year's Honours List he was rewarded with the OBE.

For England he scored 48 goals in 80 appearances, just one goal away from equalling Bobby Charlton's record. He ended his career in Japan with Nagoya Grampus Eight and now has a new career as a television personality.

Lineker's goalscoring feats had not gone unnoticed on the continent and Barcelona paid £2.3 million for his services, making him the most expensive British player in history.

There were a number of additions to the Everton squad, notably centre-half Dave Watson who arrived from Norwich City at a cost of £1 million, making him then the Blues most expensive buy.

Everton began the 1986-87 season with a number of casualties - Neville Southall, Peter Reid, Paul Bracewell, Pat van Den Hauwe, Derek Mountfield and Gary Stevens were all missing when the Blues entertained Nottingham Forest on the opening day of the campaign.

However, two goals from Kevin Sheedy gave the makeshift Everton side a 2-0 win. The Blues won four and drew three of their first seven games, suffering their first defeat at the end of September as Spurs won 2-0 at White Hart Lane. In fact, the Blues also lost their next two games against Arsenal (Home 0-1) and Charlton Athletic (Away 2-3) but by the turn of the year, they were back in contention for the Championship following six successive wins. During that sequence, the Blues scored 21 goals and conceded just one! The club's walking wounded were climbing off the treatment table and with both Cup competitions out of Everton's reach - they had lost 1-0 to Liverpool in the League Cup - the Blues could concentrate on the League Championship.

Everton knocked Arsenal off the top spot early in the New Year but Liverpool, who had moved into second place, remained most people's favourites for the title. After draws at Oxford and Manchester United, Everton lost 2-1 at Watford. These results allowed Liverpool to climb above them into top spot. As the Reds stretched their lead to nine points it looked as if the Championship race was all over. However, with Peter Reid now restored to full fitness, the Blues notched up seven victories in succession, the last being a 3-0 home win over Newcastle United with Wayne Clarke netting a hat-trick. Liverpool had stumbled and had lost their winning ways and though they beat Everton 3-1 at Anfield, there was little doubt that the Blues would win the title. The League Championship trophy was handed over at Norwich City where a goal from Pat van Den Hauwe gave Everton a 1-0 win. The Blues won their remaining two games so at the end of the season, the top of the table looked like this:

A Concise Post-War History of Everton

	P.	W.	D.	L.	F.	A.	Pts
Everton	42	26	8	8	76	31	86
Liverpool	42	23	8	11	72	42	77
Tottenham Hotspur	42	21	8	13	68	43	71

It was Everton's second title win under Howard Kendall but on 19 June 1987, the Blues lost one of the finest managers in their history when he left to take over the reins of the affluent Spanish club Athletico Bilbao. Kendall was succeeded by his number two and former colleague, Colin Harvey.

Unfortunately the 1987-88 season proved to be an immense disappointment with Harvey unable to bring further success to Goodison Park. Although he was able to keep together the previous season's title-winning squad, a number of players didn't perform to their full capability. The League title was all but surrendered by Christmas and though the Blues began the New Year with five successive victories, scoring eight goals and not conceding one, it was a little too late. The club's biggest victory during the course of the season was the 4-0 defeat of Southampton when Graeme Sharp netted all four goals. Towards the end of the campaign the Blues embarked on a ten-match unbeaten run which saw them end the season in fourth place.

Everton's dream of a fourth FA Cup Final appearance in five years was shattered by Kenny Dalglish's Liverpool side, who won 1-0 at Goodison, courtesy of a Ray Houghton goal. Earlier in the competition, Everton had needed four matches to beat Sheffield Wednesday. The first three meetings all ended 1-1 before the Blues dominated the fourth, winning 5-0 at Hillsborough with Graeme Sharp netting a hat-trick.

The club's last chance of winning some silverware disappeared in the semi-final of the League Cup when Arsenal beat the Blues 4-1 on aggregate.

The 1988-89 season saw movement off the pitch as well as on it. Gary Stevens headed a list of departures, including Alan Harper, Derek Mountfield and eventually Adrian Heath. Manager Colin Harvey decided to pin his colours to the potential of four new young faces - Stuart McCall, Pat Nevin, Neil McDonald and overshadowing the others, the £2 million purchase of Tony Cottee from West Ham United.

Surprisingly, all of them were to taste the indignity of being omitted from the manager's starting line-up during their first season with the club.

Tony Cottee made a sensational start to the season with a hat-trick on his debut in a 4-0 win over Newcastle United and a goal at Coventry the following weekend that put the Blues on top of the table. However, despite his 18 goals and a ten-match unbeaten run which raised hopes of a title charge at Christmas, Everton's Championship effort tailed away into mid-table and they ended the season in eighth place.

The Blues became a Cup team and though Bradford City knocked them out of the League Cup, they disposed of Millwall (Home 2-0), Wimbledon (Away 2-1) and Queen's Park Rangers (Home 1-0) on their way to the final of the Simod Cup.

Simod Cup Final 1989: Everton 3 Nottingham Forest 4

Both Everton and Forest contributed to a contest that was entertaining and thrilling. The Blues started the brighter of the two teams and took the lead after only eight minutes when Tony Cottee fastened on to a through ball from Trevor Steven to fire past the oncoming Sutton. Forest drew level just before half-time when Garry Parker volleyed home. Everton regained the lead shortly after the restart when Sharp lobbed the Forest 'keeper following Kevin

TREVOR STEVEN

Trevor Steven began his Football League career with Burnley, where his outstanding displays on the wing soon had the bigger clubs tracking his progress. Everton manager Howard Kendall carefully monitored the Clarets' starlet for two years before splashing out £325,000 for his services in the summer of 1983.

Although he wasn't a regular in his first season with the Blues, he collected an FA Cup winners' medal in 1984 as Everton beat Watford 2-0 in the Wembley final. The following year, Everton secured the League Championship with Steven's silky skills and tight control complementing the more aggressive, combative style of Peter Reid. In addition, the Toffees won the European Cup Winners' Cup, defeating Rapid Vienna of Austria 3-1 in the final in Rotterdam. Steven chipped in with a goal, as he had done in the deciding leg of the semi-final against Bayern Munich.

Steven had by now become a full England international, having won his first cap in the World Cup qualifier against Northern Ireland in February 1985. Like Reid, he represented England in the World Cup Finals of 1986 before returning to help Everton win the League Championship in 1986-87. After playing for Everton against Liverpool in the 1989 FA Cup Final, Steven, who had scored 58 goals in 283 games, refused to sign a new contract and joined Glasgow Rangers for £1.5 million.

With the Ibrox club he won two League Championship medals and a League Cup winners' medal but in August 1991 he was surprisingly sold to Marseille for £5.5 million.

In his only season on the Riviera, the French club won the Championship, then sold Steven back to Rangers for £2.4 million. He won two more League Championship medals, but after no longer being an automatic choice he decided to retire.

Sheedy's long ball. Southall was forced into making a couple of good saves before Forest equalised for a second time when Parker netted a marvellous individual goal. That goal took the match into extra-time and after just two minutes, Forest went into the lead for the first time as Chapman floated the ball over Southall and into the net. Everton soon drew level as Cottee converted a Pat Nevin cross and almost took the

PAT VAN DEN HAUWE

Pat Van Den Hauwe was an uncompromising, hard-tackling defender who began his Football League career with Birmingham City. When the St Andrew's club were relegated at the end of the 1983-84 season, Van Den Hauwe left to play for Everton who paid £100,000 for his services.

He made his debut in a 1-0 defeat at Arsenal in October 1984 and by the end of his first season had helped Everton win the League Championship and the European Cup Winners' Cup and won his first international cap for Wales. Although he was born in Belgium, where his father Rene had been a professional goalkeeper, he had opted out of National Service and was therefore ineligible to play for the country of his birth.

Over the next four years, Van Den Hauwe was a regular in the Everton sides which won the League Championship again in 1986-87 and reached the FA Cup Final in 1986 and 1989. Van Den Hauwe had played in 190 League and Cup games for the Toffees when in August 1989 he left Goodison to join Tottenham Hotspur for £575,000.

He finally collected an FA Cup winners' medal in May 1991 when Spurs beat Nottingham Forest and went on to play in 140 first team games for the White Hart Lane club before ending his first-class career with Millwall.

lead but Sharp's effort was tipped against the bar by Sutton. With just two minutes remaining, Chapman scored Forest's winner following good work by substitute Franz Carr.

In that season's FA Cup competition, Everton needed two matches to beat both West Bromwich Albion (Home 1-0 after a 1-1 draw) and Plymouth Argyle (Home 4-0 after a 1-1 draw) before victories over Barnsley (Away 1-0) and Wimbledon (Home 1-0) took them to a semi-final meeting with Norwich City at Villa Park. Pat Nevin scored the only goal of the game to put the Blues into the third Merseyside Cup Final to be staged at Wembley in five years.

FA Cup Final 1989: Everton 2 Liverpool 3

The game was played in an emotional atmosphere less than eight weeks after the tragedy at Hillsborough which cost 98 Liverpool fans their lives. The national stadium's perimeter fencing was taken down for the day as a mark of respect and banners proclaimed that those who could not be there would never be forgotten.

Liverpool went ahead with their very first attack of the game, Nicol and McMahon combining to set up Aldridge, whose deadly right foot shot beat Southall. The introduction of substitute Stuart McCall for the injured Bracewell pepped up Everton's attacking ideas but the break-through would just not come. With the referee about to blow for full-time, Grobbelaar could only half save Nevin's cross and McCall pounced to send the game into extra-time. The Reds, too, made a substi-tution, replacing Aldridge with Ian Rush and it was the Welsh interna-tional who beat his countrymen Ratcliffe and Southall to thump the ball into the roof of the net. McCall equalised with a powerful volley from outside the penalty area but Rush scored what proved to be the decider when he stole in to steer the ball wide of Southall after a move involv-ing Whelan and Barnes.

Rush's extra-time double not only denied Colin Harvey his first major trophy at Goodison but it also broke the age-old record of the greatest Evertonian of them all, Dixie Dean, who scored 19 goals in Merseyside derby matches - Rush, a boyhood Everton fan, had now scored 21.

After losing the opening game of the 1989-90 season, 2-0 at Coventry City, the Blues won four and drew one of their next five league games before losing 3-1 at home to Liverpool in the Merseyside derby. A few weeks later the Blues were beaten 6-2 at Aston Villa and results up until the return match with Liverpool were mixed. The Blues went to Anfield on the back of two wins and a draw but despite Graeme Sharp netting an early goal for the Goodison club, the Reds won 2-1. Everton then lost just two of their next 11 league games, recording emphatic 4-0 victories over both Crystal Palace and Nottingham Forest, but after failing to win in any of their three remaining games, had to be content with a final position of sixth.

In the FA Cup the Blues played seven matches yet didn't get past the fifth round. It took three matches to dispose of Middlesbrough (Home 1-0 after 0-0 and 1-1 draws) before two goals from Norman Whiteside accounted for Sheffield Wednesday at Hillsborough. In the fifth round the Blues went down after extra-time 2-1 at Oldham Athletic after the earlier matches had produced a 2-2 and a 1-1 draw.

At the start of the 1990-91 season the talk around Goodison was of relegation rather than of hitting the heights. It took the Blues until the seventh game of the season before they recorded their first victory, a 3-0 home defeat of Southampton, although Tony Cottee had netted a hat-trick in a 5-0 League Cup win at Wrexham four days earlier. Despite winning the return leg with the Robins 6-0, with Graeme Sharp scoring a hat-trick, after ten league games, the Blues were unable to lift themselves out of the bottom three places in Division One. This signalled an end to Colin Harvey's reign as Everton manager. Following much speculation over his successor, Howard Kendall was surprisingly brought back to Goodison from Manchester City. Kendall's first appointment was Harvey, who returned as chief coach!

Their partnership began to improve results on the field once again, breathing new life into the club. Following three victories in seven days over the Christmas period - Aston Villa (Home 1-0), Derby County (Home 2-0) and Chelsea (Away 2-1) - the Blues lifted themselves up the table to 11th position. During the New Year, Everton maintained their mid-table league position with 2-0 wins over Manchester United, Sunderland and Manchester City. The numerous other cup competitions began to affect the club's league performances and limited their rise up the table to a final position of ninth.

PAUL BRACEWELL

Paul Bracewell began his career with Stoke City, playing for three seasons with the Potters before following manager Alan Durban to Sunderland for £250,000. Things didn't work out for him at Roker Park and after just one season, he moved to Everton.

He has the rare distinction of his making his Everton debut at Wembley when he played in the Charity Shield showpiece against Liverpool in August 1984.

Forming a good understanding with Peter Reid in the Everton midfield, he won his first England cap when he replaced Bryan Robson against West Germany on the summer tour to Mexico.

On New Year's Day 1986, Bracewell suffeed a serious ankle injury in a 2-2 draw at Newcastle United and was out of action for more than 20 months. During this time, he underwent five operations and, after returning to first team action towards the end of the 1987-88 season, was forced to undergo even more surgery on his right ankle.

He had appeared in 135 games for Everton, winning League Championship and European Cup Winners' Cup medals, when in 1989 he rejoined Sunderland for a fee of £250,000.

He played for the Wearsiders in the 1992 FA Cup Final before joining Newcastle United. He made a telling contribution to the Magpies' promotion to the Premier League before, in the summer of 1995, returning to Roker Park for a third spell with Sunderland.

His experience proved vital as the Wearsiders won the First Division Championship. Bracewell later managed Fulham but lost his job towards the end of the 1999-2000 season.

DAVE WATSON

Dave Watson started his career with Liverpool but the due to the consistency of central defenders Alan Hansen and Phil Thompson, he couldn't break into the first team and moved to Norwich City for a fee of £50,000 plus another £50,000 after 25 appearances. This fee was to be doubled if he won an England cap, which he did in the summer of 1984 in the historic win over Brazil.

Everton had wanted him in the summer of 1985 but they had to wait another year to get their man. Howard Kendall paid £900,000 for Watson's services and he made his debut in a 2-0 home win over Nottingham Forest on the opening day of the 1986-87 season.

He soon formed a very effective central defensive partnership with Kevin Ratcliffe, which lasted until 1991 when the Welshman gave way to Martin Keown.

In his first season at Goodison Park, Watson helped the Blues to win their second League Championship within three years and he also won an FA Cup runners-up medal in 1989 when Everton went down to Liverpool. Having assumed the captaincy in succession to Kevin Ratcliffe in 1992, Watson led the Toffees to their FA Cup success in 1995, being voted Man-of-the-Match in their 1-0 win over Manchester United.

Dave Watson has scored many goals in over 500 games and still remains vital to the Goodison Park club's cause.

A Concise Post-War History of Everton

In the FA Cup, the Blues had tight victories over Charlton Athletic (Away 2-1) and non-League Woking (Home 1-0) before being drawn against Liverpool. In an even contest at Anfield the efforts of both teams were cancelled out and the game consequently finished in a goalless draw. The replay three days later displayed all that is good in British football. Peter Beardsley, who was later to wear the royal blue shirt, fired Liverpool in front before two minutes into the second-half, Graeme Sharp levelled the scores when he converted a cross from the overlapping Hinchcliffe. Beardsley struck again in the 70th minute but three minutes later, Sharp was presented with the easiest of tap-ins after Grobbelaar collided with Steve Nicol. Rush headed the Reds in front but as time ran out, Tony Cottee, who'd been on just minutes as a substitute for Pat Nevin, cracked a last gasp equaliser. In extra-time, John Barnes bent a free-kick into the top corner of Southall's net before Cottee struck again with just three minutes left to play. Later referred to as a 'pulsating 4-4 classic', the second replay was decided by a rare Dave Watson goal. In the quarter-finals, the Blues were outclassed and beaten 2-1 by Second Division West Ham United.

In the Zenith Data Systems Cup, Everton saw off Blackburn Rovers (Away 4-1), Sunderland (Home 4-1), with Tony Cottee scoring all the club's goals, and Barnsley (Away 1-0) to reach the Northern Area final. A few days after beating Barnsley, the Blues took a big step towards Wembley by earning a 3-3 draw against Leeds United at Elland Road. They then won the home leg of the Northern final but it was a near thing. One down at half-time, they equalised in the second-half and added two more in extra-time to beat Leeds 3-1. Their opponents at Wembley were Crystal Palace.

Zenith Data Cup Final 1991: Everton 1 Crystal Palace 4

In a fairly muscular match, Palace went ahead through a Geoff Thomas header after 66 minutes but three minutes later, Robert Warzycha eiqualised. Both sides nearly scored in the remaining minutes but the game went to extra-time. Ian Wright dazzled for Palace, scoring twice and setting up another for John Salako to give the Londoners the Cup. Unlucky Everton returned to Merseyside as losers for the fifth time in a row in Wembley finals.

With only one win in their opening eight league games, the Blues

85

made a disappointing start to the 1991-92 season before winning seven games out 15 before the turn of the year. Included in those victories were hat-tricks by Peter Beardsley (Coventry City, Home 3-0) and Tony Cottee (Tottenham Hotspur, Home 3-1).

In the New Year, results began to drop off and in an attempt to lead the club forward, manager Howard Kendall began to sever his links with the recent past, selling such stalwarts as Graeme Sharp and Kevin Sheedy. With only Peter Beardsley finding the net on a regular basis, the Blues won only five of their 19 matches after the turn of the year, finishing the season in 12th place.

During the 1992-93 season, Howard Kendall was under constant pressure to either win a trophy or tender his resignation. As it turned out neither happened as Everton struggled to find any consistency in the newly-formed Premier League.

A disastrous early season showing sent the Blues plummeting to the foot of the table. One of the major problems for the Toffees was scoring goals. Despite the continuing presence of the mercurial Peter Beardsley, the form of the club's other strikers, Paul Rideout, Maurice Johnston and Tony Cottee, was initially very disappointing. In November, Cottee had an acrimonious bust-up with Kendall and the Blues were nestling uncomfortably one off the foot of the table with only two wins from 14 games. The dismal run continued throughout the rest of November and December, during which time, in the match against Queen's Park Rangers, Everton had both Neville Southall and Paul Rideout sent-off in a 4-2 defeat. Southall also received his marching orders a couple of months later in a 3-1 reversal at Sheffield Wednesday.

The New Year brought a depressing FA Cup defeat at home to Wimbledon but there was a slight improvement in league form. By that time, the Blues had succumbed to a 1-0 home defeat at the hands of league leaders Norwich City, but some of the damage had been repaired by a rise in League status to mid-table mediocrity. But then an alarming decline in results, which included four successive defeats in February, sent Everton crashing back down the table and relegation seemed a distinct possibility.

The departure of Martin Keown to Arsenal for £2 million did little to help the Goodison crisis, though the form of major summer signing

PAT NEVIN

Glasgow-born Pat Nevin began his career with Clyde before coming south of the border to play for Chelsea in the summer of 1983, the Stamford Bridge club paying £95,000 for his services. His early form for the London club led to him winning the first of 28 international caps for Scotland against Romania in 1986. He had scored 42 goals in 227 games for Chelsea when he left to join Everton in the summer of 1988. The two clubs were unable to agree on the size of the transfer fee and so the matter was placed before an independent tribunal which fixed the fee at £925,000.

Nevin's early days at Goodison were testing, for in only his third game he damaged his knee ligaments and was sidelined for three

months. Frustrated at being out of the side, he tried to come back too early and was sidelined once again, but by the end of the season he had returned and scored vital goals in two Cup semi-finals. He went on to play in 138 games for the Toffees, scoring 20 goals before moving across the Mersey to play for Tranmere Rovers.

In five seasons with the Prenton Park club, Nevin only missed a handful of games and though not a prolific scorer, he netted a hat-trick in a 5-1 League Cup win over Oxford United. A PFA Chairman, who scored 39 goals in 239 games, was a great ambassador for Tranmere before leaving the club to play for Kilmarnock.

Barry Horne, coupled with a return to goal-scoring form by Tony Cottee, helped cushion the blow. It was Cottee who plundered a hatful of goals in the closing stages of the season that provided the necessary momentum to propel the Blues out of relegation danger and up to 13th place, compensating for League and FA Cup disappointments.

The close season brought no new players to Goodison, although Howard Kendall was constantly linked with a host of quality players who became available but no new signatures were completed.

The 1993-94 season started brightly for Everton when a 2-0 win at Southampton on the opening day of the campaign and wins over Manchester City (Home 1-0) and Sheffield United (Home 4-2), in which Tony Cottee netted a hat-trick, lifted the Blues to the top of the table. But then three consecutive defeats set the tone for a season in which Everton slid towards the foot of the table. Three back-to-back wins at the beginning of September, including a 2-0 home win over Liverpool, helped to halt the decline but the end of the month saw the Blues beaten 5-1 at home by Norwich City! The months of October and November brought just one win out of eight matches and this, coupled with a 2-0 League Cup defeat at the hands of Manchester United, brought an angry response from the Everton fans. December was even worse, for after completing the double over Southampton with a 1-0 home win, the Blues suffered four defeats.

Manager Howard Kendall was unable to bring success back to Goodison Park and decided to quit. Coach Jimmy Gabriel took over as caretaker-manager but he too could do little to revitalise a very dejected squad.

The Blues' new manager was Mike Walker, who arrived from Norwich in January 1994 in the middle of contract negotiations - Everton were later penalised by the Football League for 'poaching'. Walker's first game in charge produced a 1-1 draw at Bolton in the third round of the FA Cup but his first league game saw Tony Cottee score his second hat-trick of the season as Swindon Town were crushed 6-2 at Goodison. Sadly, the new mood of optimism was short-lived as the Blues crashed out of the FA Cup four days later, beaten 3-2 at home by Bolton.

The position in the club's boardroom, with both Bill Kenwright and Peter Johnson hoping to take control of the club, meant that little money

TONY COTTEE

Tony Cottee made a sensational first team debut for West Ham United when, at the age of 17, he scored after 26 minutes of the match against Tottenham Hotspur on New Year's Day 1983. During the 1985-86 season, he was capped by England at Under-21 level and won the PFA 'Young Player of the Year' award. Forming good striking partnerships with Paul Goddard and later Frank McAvennie, Cottee was rewarded with a full international debut for England against Sweden in September 1986. Returning to Upton Park, he scored two hat-tricks in the space of three days and ended the season as top-scorer with 22 goals. He left Upton Park in the summer of 1988, join-ing Everton for a club record fee of £2.3 million.

He quickly settled into the Toffees' side and marked his debut with a stunning hat-trick in a 4-0 win over Newcastle United on the open-ing day of the 1988-89 season. Although there were occasions when

his team-mates didn't play to his strengths, he ended his first three seasons at the club as Everton's leading goalscorer. Cottee regularly found himself at odds with his manager and in August 1989 he was fined £5,000 after refusing to turn out in a reserve team fixture. He went on to score 99 goals in 241 games for Everton before rejoining the Hammers in September 1994. He had scored 145 goals for West Ham when he was sold to Selengor. He eventually returned to the Premiership with Leicester City and continues to find the net on a regular basis.

was available to strengthen the squad.

Prior to Mike Walker's appointment the Blues had taken just one point from their previous seven matches but two wins and two draws moved them out of the relegation dog-fight. However, following a 2-1 defeat at Anfield in the Merseyside derby, the Blues picked up just five points from the next nine games, leaving them third from bottom of the Premier League with just one game remaining. Everton's opponents on the final day of the season were Wimbledon. The Blues went two-nil down at home to the Dons before recovering to win 3-2 with an 81st minute winner by Graham Stuart. Just nine minutes away from relegation, Stuart's goal maintained Everton's 40-year run in the top flight of English football.

Despite investing £3 million in Nigerian international Daniel Amokachi, who scored on his home debut in a 2-2 draw against Queen's Park Rangers, Everton had to wait until 1 November 1994 before recording their first win of the season. Prior to that they endured a run of four games without a goal and suffered heavy defeats at Manchester City (0-4) and Blackburn Rovers (0-3).

The League Cup provided no solace for manager Mike Walker as the Blues fell at the first hurdle to Division One side Portsmouth. The Everton manager tried to arrest the slide by swapping David Burrows for Tony Cottee and signing Iain Durrant and Duncan Ferguson on loan from Rangers.

November proved to be the turning point in Everton's season but despite beating West Ham United 1-0 in what was their 13th game of the 1994-95 season, thus being the last club in England to record a league win, Mike Walker was sacked after less than ten months at Goodison Park. Walker's exit paved the way for the return of Joe Royle.

He took over the club with the Blues bottom of the Premiership but a 2-0 home win over Liverpool lifted the club off the foot of the table and, with an eight-match unbeaten run, Everton edged their way out of the bottom four.

The Blues set a new club record with seven successive clean sheets starting with the 1-0 win over West Ham before Sheffield Wednesday devastated that statistic with a 4-1 win at Goodison on Boxing Day. The Blues ended the year with a 4-1 defeat of Ipswich Town, with Paul

Rideout netting two of the goals, but a failure to win two consecutive matches from the turn of the year onwards kept the club perilously close to the relegation zone. Even so, good wins were recorded over Manchester United (Home 1-0) and Newcastle United (Home 2-0) before a Paul Rideout goal gave the Blues a 1-0 win at Ipswich Town that not only completed the double over the Suffolk club but also secured Everton's place in the Premiership and a final position of 15th.

Everton began their FA Cup campaign with a third round tie at home to Derby County, winning 1-0 through an Andy Hinchcliffe goal. Hinchcliffe had earned a reputation for supplying the deadliest corner-kicks in the country. Matt Jackson's first goal for almost two years accounted for Bristol City in round four before the Blues thrashed Norwich City 5-0 at Goodison in the fifth round - with five different scorers getting in on the act. Veteran defender Dave Watson put the Blues through to their 23rd semi-final when his second-half goal defeated Newcastle United. With a powerful performance and two late goals from substitute Daniel Amokachi, Everton beat Tottenham Hotspur 4-1 in the semi-final at Elland Road to reach Wembley, where their opponents were Manchester United.

FA Cup Final 1995: Everton 1 Manchester United 0

Six days prior to the final, United had lost the Championship to Blackburn Rovers by a solitary point when they failed to beat West Ham at Upton Park. But at Wembley they were facing an Everton side that had flirted with relegation right up to the end of April. However, from the kick-off it was obvious that this was to be a keenly-contested final.

Despite wave after wave of United attacks, it was Everton who broke the deadlock. In the 30th minute, Anders Limpar and Paul Rideout quickly counter-attacked from deep in Everton's half to catch the United midfield and defence napping. Although there were four blue shirts against two red, it required an inspired piece of football from Paul Rideout to make their advantage count. When Graham Stuart's shot hit the crossbar, Peter Schmeichel was caught in no-man's land. But before he had time to react to the rebound, Rideout had nodded the ball past him.

No matter how hard they tried, United could not find a way past a determined Everton defence. Neville Southall was in outstanding form.

A double save in the 76th minute from Paul Scholes epitomised United's misery as the Blues hung on for a famous victory.

Before the start of the 1995-96 league campaign, a second-half goal by Vinny Samways against Blackburn Rovers at Wembley took the FA Charity Shield to Merseyside. Hopes were high that this would be Everton's year and to a certain degree those expectations were met as the Blues attained their highest league position for six years and their best points total for eight years.

Joe Royle was conspicuous by his absence in the transfer market during the close season but one major signing that he did complete was the £5 million transfer of Andrei Kanchelskis from Manchester United.

Everton were goalless in their opening two league matches before scoring twice in each of their next four games, but it was a generally low key first couple of months to the campaign with just two games being won, which left the Blues down in 16th place. The club's season eventually took off in November when wins over Blackburn Rovers (Home 1-0), arch rivals Liverpool (Away 2-1) and Queen's Park Rangers (Home 2-0) lifted Everton into 11th position. Three more consecutive victories over the festive period took the Blues into the top-half of the table. A final flourish of four wins, a draw and just one defeat in their last six games, including an Andrei Kanchelskis hat-trick in a 5-2 win at Sheffield Wednesday, left Everton in sixth place. The Blues would have secured a place in the UEFA Cup had Arsenal not scored a couple of late goals against Bolton on the last day of the season.

The Blues were knocked out of the League Cup when Millwall, after being held at home, won 4-2 at Goodison. Everton's first appearance in European football for eleven years saw Icelandic side Reykjavik overcome 6-3 on aggregate after a struggle in the first round. Feyenoord gained a goalless draw at Goodison in round two before the Dutch completed the task on home soil, beating the Blues 1-0.

Everton's grip on the FA Cup was shaky right from the start with Stockport County falling to a last minute John Ebbrell goal in a replay, whilst in the fourth round it was Port Vale's turn to score a last minute goal to force a replay which the First Division side won 2-1 at Vale Park.

During the close season, manager Joe Royle made a number of minor adjustments to the side, signing Paul Gerrard from Oldham Athletic for

ANDY HINCHCLIFFE

Andy Hinchcliffe began his career with Manchester City, making his league debut against Plymouth Argyle in August 1987. He played a prominent part in the Maine Road club's promotion to the First Division the following season, scoring five times from the left-back position. During the summer of 1990, he was transferred to Everton in exchange for Neil Pointon and a large cash adjustment in City's favour.

He made his debut for the Toffees in a 3-2 home defeat at the hands of Leeds United on the opening day of the 1990-91 season. Once regarded as one of the most promising left-backs in the country, Hinchcliffe was only an occasional performer in his early days at Goodison but when Joe Royle arrived in 1994, he was switched to a midfield role wide on the left and his game was transformed. His brilliant crossing and dead-ball play was a key to the Blues' FA Cup success in 1995.

Hinchcliffe's form won him recognition at full international level when he won the first of seven caps against Moldova. Injuries forced him to miss much of the 1996-97 season and in January 1998, after scoring eight goals in 219 games, he was transferred to Sheffield Wednesday for £2.85 million.

Since his arrival at Hillsborough, Hinchcliffe, whose wholehearted and enthusiastic approach is greatly appreciated by Wednesday fans, has continued to show how well suited he is to the modern wing-back position.

93

£1 million and Welsh international Gary Speed from Leeds United for £3.5 million. The Blues kicked-off the 1996-97 season with a 2-0 win at Goodison Park over Newcastle United. Speed marked his debut with a goal after David Unsworth had opened the scoring from the penalty-spot. Four days later, Duncan Ferguson scored twice in a 2-2 draw at Manchester United, they were the first goals United had conceded at Old Trafford in the Premiership in 1996. Another point was taken from Tottenham in the next match but then the Blues had a run of poor results which coincided with a humiliating defeat in the League Cup at the hands of Third Division York City, who beat Everton 4-3 on aggregate!

The Blues soon bounced back and in November, after recording their biggest-ever Premiership win, beating Southampton 7-1 with Speed netting a hat-trick, they moved up to sixth in the table. Much of the improvement was down to Nick Barmby, who had joined the club at the end of October from Middlesbrough for £5.25 million. After he had scored the winner at Derby, the Blues drew with Chelsea and Leeds before capitualting to six consecutive defeats. Such was the club's dramatic slump that there was always the possibility of them slipping into the bottom three. A Dave Watson goal helped Everton perform the double over Derby County but following the Blues 2-0 defeat at home to Manchester United, manager Joe Royle left the club by mutual consent, though it was thoght that he had disagreed with the chairman over possible moves in the transfer market.

Dave Watson, the Blues' long-serving centre-half, then accepted the dual responsibility of player-manager but in the remaining seven games of the season, the club picked up just six points to end the campaign in 15th place.

The fact that Everton lacked a permanent manager did not stop the club from splashing out £4.5 million on West Ham United defender Slaven Bilic.

In June 1997, Howard Kendall was appointed Everton manager for the third time. Of course he had enjoyed great success during the previous decade but a second spell in the early 90s was far less profitable.

Everton kicked off the 1997-98 season with three successive home games but despite Duncan Ferguson scoring for the Blues in the opening game against Crystal Palace, they went down to a 2-1 defeat. Goals by the soon departing Speed and Stuart saw off West Ham United but when Manchester United won 2-0 at Goodison, the writing was on the wall for another season of struggle. Though the club were unbeaten for the next three home games, their form away from home was nothing short of disastrous.

A sequence of five consecutive defeats begun at Goodison Park on 1 November when Southampton won 2-0 and ended 27 days later with a similar result at home to Tottenham Hotspur - this sequence saw Everton plummet from 16th to bottom of the Premiership. In the match against Leicester City at Filbert Street in mid-December, Speed's last-minute penalty ended an inglorious run of one year and four days without a victory on opposition turf!

With just one defeat from the next nine games, including victories over fellow strugglers Bolton Wanderers (Home 3-2) and Crystal Palace (Away 3-1), the Blues rose to 15th, some five points clear of the bottom three. But sadly, it was a false dawn as Kendall's side could only muster two wins from their remaining 15 games. If the club could have won just one of their last three matches, it would probably have guaranteed their safety but their survival yet again went to the wire after defeats by Sheffield Wednesday (Home 1-3) and newly-crowned champions Arsenal (Away 0-4). In the final game of the season at home to Coventry City, Gareth Farrelly repaid his £900,000 transfer fee by scoring the game's opening goal but when the Sky Blues grabbed a late equaliser, Everton still had to rely on Bolton losing against Chelsea for their own safety to be secured.

The Blues pinned their hopes for an upturn in fortunes on the most successful manager in Scottish club football in recent years, Walter Smith. But despite spending £9.5 million on summer signings - Oliver Dacourt (£4 million from Strasbourg), David Unsworth (£3.5 million from Aston Villa) and John Collins (£2 million from Monaco), and a further £8 million on Ibrahim Bakayoko and Steve Simonsen, after a couple of months of the season the Blues were still involved in an all too familiar relegation tussle. Also, much to the fans dismay, Duncan Ferguson was sold to Newcastle United for £7 million without Walter Smith's knowledge. Ferguson's transfer was expected to result in Smith's early departure but, in fact, following the boardroom revolt the

DAVID UNSWORTH

Chorley-born defender David Unsworth made his Football League debut for Everton whilst still a trainee at Tottenham Hotspur in April 1992. Although substituting at left-back for Andy Hinchcliffe, he scored a stunning equalising goal with a first-touch volley from a corner in a 3-3 thriller. He began his career as a left-back but Everton manager Mike Walker switched him to central defence at the start of the 1994-95 campaign.

England manager Terry Venables called him into his Umbro squad after a commanding FA Cup Final performance alongside Dave Watson as the Blues beat Manchester United 1-0. He made his full international debut in the 2-1 win over Japan in June 1995.

He was voted the club's 'Player of the Season' and continued to improve over the next couple of campaigns even though he failed to add to his full England cap.

In the summer of 1997 he left Goodison to join West Ham United but after just 41 games for the Hammers he transferred the claret and blue of the Hammers for Aston Villa. He soon realsied that his former employers, Everton, also coveted his signature and after pleading with the Villa hierarchy he was allowed to join the Blues for the same £3 million fee Villa had paid the Hammers without kicking a ball!

After settling back comfortably into life at Goodison, Unsworth has, at the time of writing, scored 23 goals in 211 League and Cup games for the Blues.

manager's position was actually strengthened!

After starting the 1998-99 season with five home blank scoresheets, including a goalless draw with Liverpool, Everton's first goal at Goodison encouraged the visitors, Manchester United, to score four of their own. The drought was eventually ended in February when the Blues beat Middlesbrough 5-0 with Nicky Barmby scoring twice. Before the season was over the Blues humbled West Ham United 6-0 with Kevin Campbell, on loan from Trabzonspor, netting a hat-trick.

The arrival of Kevin Campbell at Goodison Park was Walter Smith's master-stroke, the former Arsenal and Nottingham Forest striker responding with nine goals in eight games, which ensured the club's Premiership survival as they ended the season in 14th place.

In the League Cup, the long-serving Dave Watson scored his only goal of the season during a two-legged victory over Huddersfield Town while Duncan Ferguson scored his penultimate goal for the club during an extra-time victory win over Middlesbrough, only for promotion-bound Sunderland to win a penalty shoot-out at Goodison Park in the fourth round.

Since the club won the FA Cup in 1995 they had experienced short runs in the competition but in 1998-99, Bristol City (Away 2-0) and Ipswich Town (Home 1-0) were removed before the emerging talent of Francis Jeffers got the opening goal in a 2-1 defeat of Coventry City. Newcastle United ended the Blues' interest in the competition with a 4-1 quarter-final hammering on Merseyside.

During the summer months, Walter Smith continued the restructuring of his squad with Ibrahim Bakayoko departing for Marseille while veteran and fellow Scot, Richard Gough, arrived from Nottingham Forest.

Everton began the 1999-2000 season at home to European champions Manchester United, the match ending all-square at 1-1. There followed two defeats away from home before Southampton (Home 4-1) and Wimbledon (Home 4-0) were well beaten. Though the club suffered an early exit in the League Cup at the hands of Second Division Oxford United, they bounced back in the next game, beating Liverpool at Anfield courtesy of a Kevin Campbell goal.

A 1-1 draw against Coventry City five days later took the Blues to fifth place in the Premiership, their highest position of the season.

KEVIN CAMPBELL

Kevin Campbell began his Football League career with Arsenal, making his debut for the Gunners against Everton at Goodison Park on the last day of the 1987-88 season. That season he had smashed all Arsenal goalscoring records when finding the net 59 times for the youth team, whom he helped win the FA Youth Cup.

With Merson and Smith holding down the regular striking positions in Arsenal's 1988-89 League Championship-winning season, he was loaned to Leyton Orient. After another loan spell, this time with Leicester City, he began to establish himself in the Arsenal side, playing alongside a variety of striking partners.

In 1992-93 he was a member of the victorious double Cup-winning team, scoring 14 times in 37 games, and of the European Cup Winners' Cup team, when he scored four times on route to the final. He had scored 60 goals in 233 games when, in the summer of 1995, he joined Nottingham Forest for £2.5 million, a figure set by a tribunal.

After suffering throughout his first season at the City Ground with a long-standing back problem, he opened the 1996-97 season with a hat-trick at Coventry City. Campbell had scored 35 goals in 93 games when he left Forest in the summer of 1998 to join Trabzonspor of Turkey.

After an unhappy spell he exploded back onto the Premiership scene following a loan spell with Everton. His nine goals in eight games, including a hat-trick against West Ham United, saw him end the season as Everton's top-scorer and their saviour. The object of hero worship at Goodison Park, Campbell, has now joined the club on a permanent basis.

Results over the next few weeks were mixed but following a 5-1 reversal in the return match at Old Trafford, the Blues embarked on an eight-match unbeaten run which included two victories in the FA Cup and a 5-0 mauling of Peter Reid's Sunderland side. Despite a brave performance from Second Division leaders Preston North End in the fifth round of the FA Cup, goals from David Unsworth and Joe-Max Moore took the club into the quarter-finals. The experienced striker, who had joined the Blues from American Major League side New England Revolution, netted again in the sixth round tie but visitors Aston Villa won 2-1. Everton bounced back in their next game, winning 4-0 at West Ham United with Nick Barmby scoring a hat-trick. There were a couple of good wins over Watford (Home 4-2) and Bradford City (Home 4-0) before the Blues entertained Liverpool in the 162nd Merseyside derby on Good Friday. Though the game ended goalless, every Evertonian inside Goodison Park thought the Blues had secured a dramatic injury-time winner until referee Graham Poll revealed he had already blown for full-time. Don Hutchison's unwitting deflection from Sander Westerveld's clearance rebounded straight into the Gladys Street net and sparked the briefest goal celebrations in history! The ground erupted until the match official pointed to his wristwatch.

The Blues finished the season in ninth place, a campaign in which no-one could doubt the level of commitment the players put in. Maybe 2000-2001 will see the club get that little break that they deserve!

APPENDIX

Football League career statistics of every Blackburn Rovers player
since 1945

KEY:

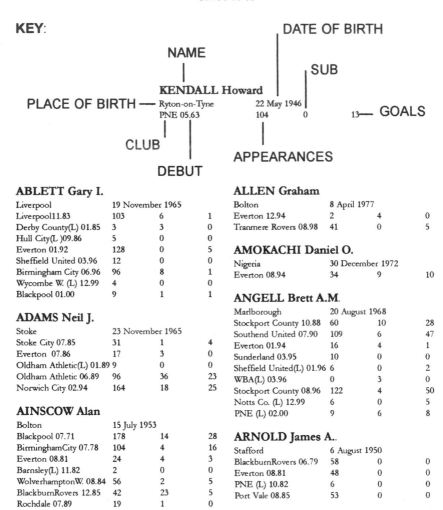

DATE OF BIRTH

NAME

SUB

KENDALL Howard

PLACE OF BIRTH — Ryton-on-Tyne   22 May 1946

PNE 05.63   104   0   13— GOALS

CLUB

APPEARANCES

DEBUT

ABLETT Gary I.

Liverpool	19 November 1965		
Liverpool 11.83	103	6	1
Derby County(L) 01.85	3	3	0
Hull City(L)09.86	5	0	0
Everton 01.92	128	0	5
Sheffield United 03.96	12	0	0
Birmingham City 06.96	96	8	1
Wycombe W. (L) 12.99	4	0	0
Blackpool 01.00	9	1	1

ADAMS Neil J.

Stoke	23 November 1965		
Stoke City 07.85	31	1	4
Everton 07.86	17	3	0
Oldham Athletic(L) 01.89	9	0	0
Oldham Athletic 06.89	96	36	23
Norwich City 02.94	164	18	25

AINSCOW Alan

Bolton	15 July 1953		
Blackpool 07.71	178	14	28
BirminghamCity 07.78	104	4	16
Everton 08.81	24	4	3
Barnsley(L) 11.82	2	0	0
WolverhamptonW. 08.84	56	2	5
BlackburnRovers 12.85	42	23	5
Rochdale 07.89	19	1	0

ALLEN Graham

Bolton	8 April 1977		
Everton 12.94	2	4	0
Tranmere Rovers 08.98	41	0	5

AMOKACHI Daniel O.

Nigeria	30 December 1972		
Everton 08.94	34	9	10

ANGELL Brett A.M.

Marlborough	20 August 1968		
Stockport County 10.88	60	10	28
Southend United 07.90	109	6	47
Everton 01.94	16	4	1
Sunderland 03.95	10	0	0
Sheffield United(L) 01.96	6	0	2
WBA(L) 03.96	0	3	0
Stockport County 08.96	122	4	50
Notts Co. (L) 12.99	6	0	5
PNE (L) 02.00	9	6	8

ARNOLD James A..

Stafford	6 August 1950		
BlackburnRovers 06.79	58	0	0
Everton 08.81	48	0	0
PNE (L) 10.82	6	0	0
Port Vale 08.85	53	0	0

A Concise Post-War History of Everton

ASHWORTH Alec

Southport	1 October 1939		
Everton 05.57	12	0	3
Luton Town 10.60	63	0	20
Northampton T. 07.62	30	0	25
Preston North End 06.63	42	11	4

ASPINALL Warren

Wigan	13 September 1967		
Wigan Athletic 08.85	39	12	22
Everton 05.86	0	7	0
Aston Villa 02.87	40	4	14
Portsmouth 08.88	97	35	21
Bournemouth(L) 08.93	4	2	1
Swansea City(L) 10.93	5	0	0
Bournemouth 12.93	26	1	8
Carlisle United 03.95	99	8	12
Brentford 11.97	41	2	5
Colchester United 02.99	22	0	5
Brighton & HA 09.99	19	12	3

ATKINS Ian L.

Birmingham	16 January 1957		
Shrewsbury Town 01.75	273	6	58
Sunderland 08.82	76	1	6
Everton 11.84	6	1	1
Ipswich Town 09.85	73	4	4
Birmingham City 03.88	98	3	6
Cambridge U.(NC) 12.92	1	1	0
Doncaster R..(NC) 01.94	7	0	0

ATTEVELD Raymond

Holland	8 September 1966		
Everton 08.89	41	10	1
West Ham Utd.(L) 02.92	1	0	0
Bristol City 03.92	9	5	1

BAILEY John A.

Liverpool	1 April 1957		
Blackburn Rovers 04.75	115	5	1
Everton 07.79	171	0	3
Newcastle United 10.85	39	1	0
Bristol City 09.88	79	1	1

BAKAYOKO Ibrahima

Seguela,IvoryCoast	31 December 1976		
Everton 10.98	17	6	4

BALL Alan J.

Farnworth	12 May 1946		
Blackpool 05.62	116	0	41
Everton 08.66	208	0	66
Arsenal 12.71	177	0	45
Southampton 12.76	132	0	9
Blackpool 07.80	30	0	5

Southampton 03.81	63	0	2
Bristol Rovers 01.83	17	0	2

BALL Michael J.

Liverpool	2 October 1979		
Everton 10.96	73	19	5

BARLOW Stuart

Liverpool	16 July 1968		
Everton 06.90	24	4	710
Rotherham Utd.(L) 01.92	0	1	0
Oldham Athletic 11.95	78	15	31
Wigan Athletic 03.98	72	11	40

BARMBY Nicholas J.

Hull	11 February 1974		
Tottenham H. 04.91	81	6	20
Middlesbrough 08.95	42	0	8
Everton 11.96	105	11	18

BARNETT Geoffrey C.

Northwich	16 October 1946		
Everton 05.64	10	0	0
Arsenal 10.69	39	0	0

BARRETT Earl D.

Rochdale	28April1967		
ManchesterCity 04.85	2	1	0
Chester City(L) 03.86	12	0	0
Oldham Athletic 11.87	181	2	7
Aston Villa 02.92	118	1	1
Everton 01.95	73	1	0
Sheffield Utd.(L) 01.98	5	0	0
Sheffield Wed. 02.98	10	5	0

BARTON John S.

Birmingham	24October1953		
Everton 12.78	18	2	0
Derby County 03.82	68	1	1

BEAGRIE Peter S.

Middlesbrough	28November1965		
Middlesbrough 09.83	24	9	2
Sheffield United 08.86	81	3	11
Stoke City 06.88	54	0	7
Everton 11.89	88	26	11
Sunderland(L) 09.91	5	0	1
Manchester City 03.94	46	6	3
Bradford City 07.97	104	8	19
Everton(L) 03.98	4	2	0

BEARDSLEY Peter A.

Newcastle	18 January 1961		
Carlisle United 08.79	93	11	22
Newcastle United 09.83	146	1	61

Liverpool 07.87	120	11	46
Everton 08.91	81	0	25
Newcastle United 07.93	126	3	47
Bolton Wanderers 08.97	14	3	2
Manchester City(L) 02.98	5	1	0
Fulham 03.98	19	2	4
Hartlepool United 12.98	22	0	2

BELFITT Roderick M.

Bournemouth	30 October 1945		
Leeds United 07.63	57	18	17
Ipswich Town 11.71	40	0	13
Everton 11.72	14	2	2
Sunderland 10.73	36		4
Fulham(L) 11.74	6	0	1
Huddersfield Town 02.75	34	0	8

BENNETT Henry S.

Liverpool	16 May 1949		
Everton 03.67	2	1	0
Aldershot 01.71	77	12	7
Crewe Alexandra 07.73	28	2	1

BENTHAM Stanley J.

Leigh	17 March 1915		
Everton 01.34	110	0	17

BENTLEY John

Liverpool	17February1942		
Everton 11.59	1	0	0
Stockport County 05.61	49	0	5

BERNARD Michael P.

Shrewsbury	10 January 1948		
Stoke City 01.65	124	12	6
Everton 04.72	139	8	8
Oldham Athletic 07.77	6	0	0

BILEY Alan P.

Leighton Buzzard	26 February 1957		
Cambridge United 07.75	160	5	75
Derby County 01.80	47	0	19
Everton 07.81	16	3	3
Stoke City(L) 03.82	8	0	1
Portsmouth 08.82	101	4	51
Brighton & HA 03.85	34	1	8
CambridgeU.(NC) 11.86	0	3	0

BILIC Slaven

Split, Croatia	11 September 1968		
West Ham United 02.96	48	0	2
Everton 07.97	26	2	0

BILLING Peter G.

Liverpool	24 October 1964		
Everton 01.86	1	0	0
Crewe Alexandra 12.86	83	5	1
Coventry City 06.89	51	7	1
Port Vale 02.93	23	3	0
Hartlepool United 08.95	35	1	0
Crewe Alexandra 08.96	9	6	0

BINGHAM William L.

Belfast	5 August 1931		
Sunderland 11.50	206	0	45
Luton Town 07.58	87	0	27
Everton 10.60	86	0	23
Port Vale 08.63	40	0	6

BIRCH Kenneth J.

Birkenhead	31 December 1933		
Everton 08.51	43	0	1
Southampton 03.58	34	0	3

BISHOP Ian W.

Liverpool	29 May 1965		
Everton 05.83	0	1	0
Crewe Alex.(L) 03.84	4	0	0
Carlisle United 10.84	131	1	14
Bournemouth 07.88	44	0	2
Manchester City 08.89	18	1	2
West Ham United 12.89	240	14	12
Manchester City 03.98	25	6	0

BORROWS Brian

Liverpool	20 December 1940		
Everton 04.80	27	0	0
Bolton Wanderers 03.83	95	0	0
Coventry City 06.85	396	13	11
Bristol City(L) 09.93	6	0	0
Swindon Town 09.97	80	0	0

BOYES Walter E.

Sheffield	5 January 1913		
WBA 02.31	151	0	35
Everton 02.38	66	0	11
Notts County 08.49	3	0	1
Scunthorpe United 08.50	13	0	2

BRACEWELL Peter

Heswall	19 July 1962		
Stoke City 02.80	123	6	5
Sunderland 07.83	38	0	4
Everton 05.84	95	0	7
Sunderland 08.89	112	1	2
Newcastle United 06.92	64	9	3
Sunderland 05.95	76	1	0
Fulham 10.97	61	1	1

A Concise Post-War History of Everton

BRAMWELL John
Ashton-in-Makerfield	1 March 1937		
Everton 04.58	52	0	0
Luton Town 10.60	187	0	1

BRANCH Michael P.
Liverpool	18 October 1978		
Everton 10.95	16	25	3
Manchester City(L) 10.98	4	0	0
Wolverhampton W. 11.99	25	2	6

BRAND Andrew S.
Edinburgh	8 November 1957		
Everton 11.75	2	0	0
Crewe Alex.(L) 02.77	14	0	0
Crewe Alex.(L) 08.78	1	0	0
Hereford United 05.80	54	0	0
Wrexham(L) 11.82	1	0	0
Blackpool(NC) 03.84	3	0	0

BRINDLE William
Liverpool	29 January 1950		
Everton 08.67	1	0	0
Barnsley 05.70	0	1	0

BROWN Alexander D.
Grangemouth	24 March 1939		
Everton 09.63	176	33	9
Shrewsbury Town 05.71	21	0	0
Southport 07.72	17	2	0

BUCKLE Edward H.
Southwark	28 October 1924		
Manchester United 11.45	20	0	6
Everton 11.49	97	0	31
Exeter City 07.55	65	0	12

BUCKLEY Michael J.
Manchester	4 November 1953		
Everton 06.71	128	7	10
Sunderland 08.78	117	4	7
Hartlepool U.(NC) 08.83	6	0	0
Carlisle United 09.83	24	1	2
Middlesbrough 06.84	27	0	0

BURNETT George G.
Liverpool	11 February 1920		
Everton 09.38	47	0	0
Oldham Athletic 10.51	100	0	0

BURROWS David
Dudley	25 October 1968		
WBA 11.86	37	9	1

Liverpool 10.88	135	11	3
West Ham United 09.93	29	0	1
Everton 09.94	19	0	0
Coventry City 03.95	106	5	0

CADAMARTERI Daniel L.
Bradford	12 October 1979		
Everton 10.96	29	45	9
Fulham (L) 11.99	3	2	1

CAMERON Daniel
Dublin	16 June 1922		
Everton 07.48	1	0	0

CAMPBELL Kevin J.
Lambeth	4 February 1970		
Arsenal 02.88	124	42	46
Leyton Orient(L) 01.89	16	0	9
Leicester City(L) 11.89	11	0	5
Nottingham Forest 07.95	79	1	32
Everton 03.99	34	0	21

CATTERICK Harry
Darlington	26 November 1919		
Everton 03.37	59	0	19
Crewe Alexandra 12.51	24	0	11

CLARKE Wayne
Wolverhampton	28 February 1961		
Wolverhampton W. 03.78	129	19	30
Birmingham City 08.84	92	0	38
Everton 03.87	46	11	18
Leicester City 07.89	10	1	1
Manchester City 01.90	7	14	2
Shrewsbury T.(L) 10.90	7	0	6
Stoke City(L) 03.91	9	0	3
Wolv'pton W.(L) 09.91	1	0	0
Walsall 07.92	39	0	21
Shrewsbury Town 08.93	53	6	22

CLELAND Alexander
Glasgow	10 December 1970		
Everton 07.98	19	8	0

CLEMENTS David
Larne	15 September 1945		
Coventry City 07.64	228	2	26
Sheffield Wed. 08.71	78	0	0
Everton 09.73	81	2	6

CLINTON Thomas J.
Dublin	13 April 1926		
Everton 03.48	73	0	4
Blackburn Rovers 04.55	6	0	0
Tranmere Rovers 06.56	9	0	0

COLLINS John A.P.
Galashiels	31 January 1968		
Everton 08.98	50	3	3

COLLINS Robert Y.
Glasgow	16 February 1931		
Everton 09.58	133	0	42
Leeds United 03.62	149	0	24
Bury 02.67	74	1	5
Oldham Athletic 10.72	6	1	0

CONNOLLY John
Barrhead	13 June 1950		
Everton 03.72	105	3	16
Birmingham City 09.76	49	8	9
Newcastle United 05.78	42	7	10

CORR Peter J.
Dundalk	22 June 1923		
Preston North End 04.47	3	0	0
Everton 08.48	24	0	2

COTTEE Anthony R.
WestHam	11 July 1965		
West Ham United 09.82	203	9	92
Everton 08.88	161	23	72
West Ham United 09.94	63	4	23
Leicester City 08.97	66	17	27
Birmingham C.(L) 11.97	4	1	1

CUMMINS George P.
Dublin	12 March 1931		
Everton 11.50	24	0	0
Luton Town 08.53	184	0	21
Hull City 11.62	21	0	2

CURRAN Edward
Hemsworth	20 March 1955		
Doncaster Rovers 07.73	67	1	11
Nottingham Forest 08.75	46	2	12
Bury(L) 10.77	2	0	0
Derby County 11.77	26	0	2
Southampton 08.78	25	1	0
Sheffield Wed. 03.79	122	3	35
Sheffield United 08.82	31	2	3
Everton(L) 12.82	7	0	1
Everton 09.83	12	5	0
Huddersfield Town 07.85	33	1	7
Hull City 10.86	4	0	0
Sunderland 11.86	9	0	1
Grimsby Town 11.87	10	2	0
Chesterfield(NC) 03.88	0	1	0

DACOURT Olivier
Paris	25 September 1974		
Everton 08.98	28	2	2

DANSKIN Jason
Winsford	28 Decembe r1967		
Everton 07.85	1	0	0
Mansfield Town 03.87	10	0	0
Hartlepool U.(L) 01.88	3	0	0

D'ARCY Francis A.
Liverpool	8 December 1946		
Everton 08.64	8	8	0
Tranmere Rovers 07.72	7	1	1

DARRACOTT Terence M.
Liverpool	6 December 1950		
Everton 07.68	138	10	0
Wrexham 09.79	22	0	0

DAVIES Dai W.
Ammanford	1 April 1948		
Swansea City 08.69	9	0	0
Everton 12.70	82	0	0
Swansea City(L) 02.74	6	0	0
Wrexham 09.77	144	0	0
Swansea City 07.81	71	0	0
Tranmere Rovers 06.83	42	0	0

DAVIES John W.
Holt	14 November 1916		
Chester City 12.34	18	0	1
Everton 07.37	1	0	0
Plymouth Argyle 02.47	33	0	0
BristolCity 05.48	30	0	1

DEGN Peter
Aarhus, Denmark	6 April 1977		
Everton 02.99	0	4	0

DOBSON Martin J.
Blackburn	14 February 1948		
Burnley 08.67	220	4	43
Everton 08.74	190	0	29
Burnley 08.79	186	0	20
Bury 03.84	60	1	4

DODDS Ephraim
Grangemouth	7 September 1915		
Sheffield United 05.34	178	0	114
Blackpool 03.39	12	0	10
Everton 11.46	55	0	36
Lincoln City 10.48	60	0	38

DONOVAN Daniel C.

Cork	23 December 1929		
Everton 05.49	179	0	2
Grimsby Town 08.58	238	0	1

DUGDALE Gordon

Liverpool	21 February 1924		
Everton 06.47	58	0	0

DUNNE Richard P.

Dublin	21 September 1979		
Everton 10.96	50	7	0

EASTHOPE Joseph D.

Liverpool	26 September 1929		
Everton 04.50	2	0	0
Stockport County 06.54	9	0	2

EASTOE Peter R.

Tamworth	2 August 1953		
WolverhamptonW. 06.71	4	2	0
Swindon Town 11.73	91	0	43
QPR 03.76	69	3	15
Everton 03.79	88	7	26
WBA 08.82	30	1	8
Leicester City(L) 10.83	5	0	1
Huddersfield T.(L) 03.84	8	2	0
Walsall(L) 08.84	6	0	1
Leicester City(L) 10.84	6	0	1
Wolv'pton W.(L) 02.85	8	0	0

EBBRELL John K.

Bromborough	1 October 1969		
Everton 11.86	207	10	13
Sheffield United 03.97	1	0	0

EGLINGTON Thomas J.

Dublin	15 January 1923		
Everton 07.46	394	0	76
Tranmere Rovers 06.57	172	0	36

FALDER David E.J.

Liverpool	21 October 1922		
Everton 12.45	25	0	0

FARLEY Adam J.

Liverpool	12 January 1980		
Everton 02.98	0	1	0

FARRALL Alec

Hoylake	3 March 1936		
Everton 03.53	5	0	0
Preston North End 05.57	27	0	9
Gillingham 07.60	202	0	19

Lincoln City 06.65	20	0	2
Watford 07.66	47	1	8

FARRELL Peter D.

Dublin	16 August 1922		
Everton 08.46	422	0	13
Tranmere Rovers 10.57	14	0	1

FARRELLY Gareth

Dublin	28 August 1975		
Aston Villa 01.92	2	6	0
Rotherham Utd(L) 03.95	9	1	2
Everton 07.97	18	9	1
Bolton Wanderers 10.99	8	3	1

FELL James I.

Grimsby	4 January 1936		
Grimsby Town 04.54	166	0	35
Everton 03.61	27	0	4
Newcastle United 03.62	49	0	16
Walsall 07.63	21	0	4
Lincoln City 01.64	63	0	10

FERGUSON Duncan

Stirling	27 December 1971		
Everton 10.94	110	6	37
NewcastleUnited 11.98	24	6	8

FERGUSON Michael J.

Newcastle	3 October 1954		
Coventry City 12.71	121	6	51
Everton 08.81	7	1	4
Birmingham City 11.82	22	0	9
Coventry City(L) 03.84	7	0	3
Brighton & HA 09.84	17	0	6
Colchester United 03.86	25	1	11

FIELDING Walter A.

Edmonton	26 November 1919		
Everton 09.45	380	0	49
Southport 01.59	20	0	1

FINNIS Harold A.

Liverpool	21 November 1920		
Everton 06.46	1	0	0

GABRIEL James

Dundee	16 October 1940		
Everton 03.60	255	1	33
Southampton 07.67	190	1	25
Bournemouth 07.72	53	0	4
Swindon Town(L) 10.73	6	0	0
Brentford 03.74	9	0	0

GANNON Michael J.

Liverpool	2 February 1943		
Everton 02.60	3	0	0
Scunthorpe United 05.62	15	0	0
Crewe Alexandra 10.64	206	4	2

GARDNER Thomas

Liverpool	17 March 1923		
Everton 06.47	1	0	0

GAULD James

Aberdeen	9 May 1929		
Charlton Athletic 05.55	47	0	21
Everton 10.56	23	0	7
Plymouth Argyle 10.57	64	0	25
Swindon Town 08.59	40	0	14
Mansfield Town 11.60	4	0	3

GEMMILL Scot

Paisley	2 January 1971		
Nottingham Forest 01.90	228	17	21
Everton 03.99	13	8	2

GERRARD Paul W.

Heywood	22 January 1973		
Oldham Athletic 11.91	118	1	0
Everton 07.96	42	1	0
Oxford United(L) 12.98	16	0	0

GIBSON David J.

Runcorn	18 March 1931		
Everton 08.50	3	0	0
Swindon Town 11.54	70	0	6

GIDMAN John

Liverpool	10 January 1954		
Aston Villa 08.71	196	1	9
Everton 10.79	64	0	2
Manchester United 08.81	94	1	4
Manchester City 10.86	52	1	1
Stoke City 08.88	7	3	0
Darlington 02.89	13	0	1

GLAZZARD James

Normanton	23 April 1923		
Huddersfield Town 10.43	299	0	141
Everton 09.56	3	0	0
Mansfield Town 12.56	21	0	10

GLOVER Gerard J.

Liverpool	27 September 1946		
Everton 08.64	2	1	0
Mansfield Town 09.67	18	1	0

GODFREY Brian C.

Flint	1 May 1940		
Everton 05.58	1	0	0
Scunthorpe United 06.60	87	0	24
Preston North End 10.63	121	1	52
Aston Villa 09.67	139	4	22
Bristol Rovers 05.71	79	2	16
Newport County 06.73	117	1	14

GOODLASS Ronald

Liverpool	6 September 1953		
Everton 07.71	31	4	2
Fulham 09.80	21	1	2
Scunthorpe United 03.82	9	0	0
Tranmere Rovers 12.83	19	2	0

GRANT Anthony J.

Liverpool	14 November 1974		
Everton 07.93	43	18	2
Swindon Town(L) 01.96	3	0	1
Tranmere R. (L) 09.99	8	1	0
Manchester City 12.99	4	4	0

GRANT John A.

Gateshead	8 September 1924		
Everton 12.42	121	0	10
Rochdale 05.56	102	0	3
Southport 01.59	40	0	0

GRAY Andrew M.

Glasgow	30 November 1955		
AstonVilla 10.75	112	1	54
Wolverhampton W. 09.79	130	3	38
Everton 11.83	44	5	14
Aston Villa 07.85	53	1	5
Notts County(L) 08.87	3	1	0
WBA 09.87	32	3	10

GREEN Colin R.

Wrexham	10 February 1942		
Everton 02.59	15	0	1
Birmingham City 12.62	183	0	1
Wrexham(L) 01.71	3	0	0

GREENHALGH Norman

Bolton	10 August 1914		
New Brighton 10.35	77	0	8
Everton 01.38	106	0	1

GRIFFITHS Bryan

Liverpool	21 November 1938		
Everton 03.56	2	0	0
Southport 06.60	117	0	1

A Concise Post-War History of Everton

HAMILTON Bryan

Belfast	21 December 1946		
Ipswich Town 08.71	142	11	43
Everton 11.75	38	3	5
Millwall 07.77	48	1	6
Swindon Town 11.78	19	5	1
Tranmere Rovers 10.80	95	14	0

HAMPSON Alan

Prescot	31 December 1927		
Everton 08.49	1	0	0
Halifax Town 11.52	121	0	32
Bradford City 07.56	6	0	4

HARBURN Peter A.P.

Shoreditch	18 June 1931		
Brighton & HA 02.56	126	0	61
Everton 8.58	4	0	1
Scunthorpe United 01.59	20	0	8
Workington 10.59	67	0	23

HARPER Alan

Liverpool	1 November 1960		
Everton 06.83	103	24	4
Sheffield Wed. 07.88	32	3	0
Manchester City 12.89	46	4	1
Everton 08.91	45	6	0
Luton Town 09.93	40	1	1
Burnley 08.94	30	1	0
Cardiff City(L) 11.95	5	0	0

HARPER Joseph M.

Greenock	11 January 1948		
Huddersfield Town 03.67	26	2	4
Everton 12.72	40	3	12

HARRIS Albert E.

Bootle	21 November 1931		
Everton 01.55	5	0	0
Tranmere Rovers 05.57	33	0	0
Southport 07.60	159	0	0

HARRIS Brian

Bebington	16 May 1935		
Everton 01.54	310	0	23
Cardiff City 10.66	147	2	0
Newport County 07.71	85	0	0

HARRIS James

Birkenhead	18 August 1933		
Everton 09.51	191	0	65
Birmingham City 12.60	93	0	37
Oldham Athletic 07.64	28	1	9

HARRIS Joseph A.

Liverpool	20 September 1926		
Everton 07.50	14	0	4

HARTFORD Asa R.

Clydebank	24 October 1950		
WBA 11.67	206	8	18
Manchester City 08.74	184	1	22
Nottingham Forest 07.79	3	0	0
Everton 08.79	81	0	6
Manchester City 10.81	75	0	7
Norwich City 10.84	28	0	2
Bolton Wanderers 07.85	81	0	8
Stockport County 06.87	42	3	0
Oldham Athletic 03.89	3	4	0
Shrewsbury Town 08.89	22	3	0

HARVEY Colin J.

Liverpool	16 November 1944		
Everton 10.62	317	3	18
Sheffield Wed. 09.74	45	0	2

HAUGHEY William

Glasgow	20 December 1932		
Everton 06.56	4	0	1

HEARD Patrick T.

Hull	17 March 1960		
Everton 03.78	10	1	0
Aston Villa 10.79	20	4	2
Sheffield Wed. 01.83	22	3	3
Newcastle United 09.84	34	0	2
Middlesbrough 08.85	25	0	2
Hull City 03.86	79	1	5
Rotherham United 07.88	41	3	7
Cardiff City 08.90	45	1	4
Hull City (NC) 08.92	3	1	0

HEATH Adrian P.

Stoke	11 January 1961		
Stoke City 01.79	94	1	16
Everton 01.82	206	20	71
Aston Villa 08.89	8	1	0
Manchester City 02.90	58	17	4
Stoke City 03.92	5	1	0
Burnley 08.92	109	6	29
Sheffield United 12.95	0	4	0
Burnley (NC) 03.96	1	4	0

HEDLEY John R.

Willington Quay	11 December 1923		
Everton 04.45	54	0	0
Sunderland 08.50	269	0	0
Gateshead 07.59	11	0	0

The Toffees

HESLOP George W.
Wallsend	1 July 1940		
Newcastle United 02.59	27	0	0
Everton 03.62	10	0	0
Manchester City 09.65	159	3	1
Bury 08.72	37	0	0

HICKSON David
Salford	30 October 1929		
Everton 05.48	139	0	63
Aston Villa 09.55	12	0	1
Huddersfield Town 11.55	54	0	28
Everton 08.57	86	0	32
Liverpool 11.59	60	0	37
Bury 01.62	8	0	0
Tranmere Rovers 08.62	45	0	21

HIGGINS Mark N.
Buxton	29 September 1958		
Everton 08.76	150	2	6
Manchester United 12.85	6	0	0
Bury 01.87	67	1	0
Stoke City 09.88	37	2	1

HIGGINS William C.
Birkenhead	26 February 1924		
Everton 03.46	48	0	8

HILL James M.
Carrickfergus	31 October 1935		
Newcastle United 07.57	11	0	2
Norwich City 07.58	161	0	55
Everton 08.63	7	0	1
Port Vale 10.65	63	0	8

HILLS John D.
Blackpool	21 April 1978		
Everton 11.95	1	2	0
Swansea City (L) 01.97	11	0	0
Swansea City (L) 08.97	7	0	0
Blackpool 01.98	46	1	2

HINCHCLIFFE Andrew G.
Manchester	5 February 1969		
Manchester City 06.86	107	5	8
Everton 07.90	170	12	6
Sheffield Wed. 01.98	76	0	5

HODGE Martin J.
Southport	4 February 1959		
Plymouth Argyle 02.77	43	0	0
Everton 07.79	25	0	0
PNE (L) 12.81	28	0	0
Oldham Ath. (L) 07.82	4	0	0
Gillingham (L) 01.83	4	0	0

PNE (L) 02.83	16	0	0
Sheffield Wed. 08.83	197	0	0
Leicester City 08.88	75	0	0
Hartlepool United 08.91	69	0	0
Rochdale 07.93	42	0	0
Plymouth Argyle 08.94	17	0	0

HOLMES Paul
Stocksbridge	18 February 1968		
Doncaster Rovers 02.86	42	5	1
Torquay United 08.88	127	11	4
Birmingham City 06.92	12	0	0
Everton 03.93	21	0	0
WBA 01.96	102	1	1

HORNE Barry
St Asaph	18 May 1962		
Wrexham 06.84	136	0	16
Portsmouth 07.87	66	4	7
Southampton 03.89	111	1	6
Everton 07.92	118	5	3
Birmingham City 06.96	33	0	0
Huddersfield Town 10.97	55	9	1
Sheffield Wed. 03.00	7	0	0

HOTTIGER Marc
Switzerland	7 November 1967		
Newcastle United 08.94	38	1	1
Everton 03.96	13	4	1

HUGHES Darren J.
Prescot	6 October 1965		
Everton 10.83	3	0	0
Shrewsbury Town 06.85	34	3	1
Brighton & HA 09.86	26	0	2
Port Vale 09.87	183	1	4
Northampton T. 01.95	19	2	0
Exeter City 11.95	58	4	1

HUGHES Mark L.
Wrexham	1 November 1963		
Manchester United 11.80	85	4	37
Manchester United 07.88	251	5	82
Chelsea 07.95	88	7	25
Southampton 07.98	32	0	1
Everton 03.00	9	0	1

HUGHES Stephen J.
Reading	18 September 1976		
Arsenal 07.95	21	26	4
Everton 03.00	11	0	1

HUMPHREYS Gerald
Llandudno	14 January 1946		
Everton 09.63	12	0	2

108

Crystal Palace 06.70	4	7	0
Crewe Alexandra 01.72	184	9	30

HUMPHREYS John V.

Llandudno	13 January 1920		
Everton 04.43	53	0	0

HUNT ROGER (ERNIE) P.

Swindon	17 March 1943		
Swindon Town 03.60	214	0	82
Wolverhampton W.09.65	74	0	32
Everton 09.67	12	2	3
Coventry City 03.68	140	6	45
Doncaster Rov.(L) 01.73	9	0	1
Bristol City 12.73	9	3	?

HURST John

Blackpool	6 February 1947		
Everton 10.64	336	11	29
Oldham Athletic 06.76	169	1	2

HUSBAND James

Newcastle	15 October 1947		
Everton 10.64	158	7	44
Luton Town 11.73	138	5	44

HUTCHISON Donald

Gateshead	9 May 1971		
Hartlepool United 03.90	19	5	3
Liverpool 11.90	33	12	7
West Ham United 08.94	30	5	11
Sheffield United 01.96	70	8	5
Everton 02.98	68	7	10

IRVINE Alan J.

Glasgow	12 July 1958		
Everton 05.81	51	9	4
Crystal Palace 08.84	108	1	12
Blackburn Rovers 10.89	40	18	3

IRVING David

Cockermouth	10 September 1951		
Workington 05.70	57	816	
Everton 01.73	4	2	0
Sheffield United 09.75	0	2	0
Oldham Athletic 06.76	18	3	7

JACK Ross J.

Inverness	21 March 1959		
Everton 02.77	1	0	1
Norwich City 12.79	31	25	10
Lincoln City 08.83	52	816	

JACKSON George

Liverpool	14 January 1911		
Everton 05.32	75	0	0

JACKSON Matthew A.

Leeds	19 October 1971		
Luton Town 07.90	7	2	0
PNE (L) 03.91	3	1	0
Everton 10.91	132	6	4
Charlton Ath. (L)03.96	8	0	0
QPR (L) 08.96	7	0	0
Birmingham C. (L) 10.96	10	0	0
Norwich City 12.96	132	3	6

JACKSON Thomas

Belfast	3 November 1946		
Everton 02.68	30	2	0
Nottingham Forest 10.70	73	8	6
Manchester United 07.75	18	1	0

JEFFERS Francis

Liverpool	25 January 1981		
Everton 02.98	27	10	12

JEVONS Philip

Liverpool	1 August 1979		
Everton 11.97	1	1	0

JOHNSON Albert

Morpeth	7 September 1923		
Everton 05.39	9	0	0
Chesterfield 09.48	19	0	1

JOHNSON David E.

Liverpool	23 October 1951		
Everton 04.69	47	3	11
Ipswich Town 11.72	134	3	35
Liverpool 08.76	128	20	55
Everton 08.82	32	8	4
Barnsley (L) 02.84	4	0	1
Manchester City 03.84	4	2	1
PNE 10.84	20	4	3

JOHNSON Thomas

Newcastle	15 January 1971		
Notts County 01.89	100	18	47
Derby County 03.92	91	7	30
Aston Villa 01.95	38	19	13
Everton (L) 09.99	0	3	0

JOHNSTON Maurice J.G.

Glasgow	30 April 1963		
Watford 11.83	37	1	23
Everton 11.91	28	6	10

The Toffees

JONES David R.
Liverpool	17 August 1956		
Everton 05.74	79	7	1
Coventry City 06.79	8	3	0
PNE 08.83	50	0	1

JONES Gary K.
Prescot	5 January 1951		
Everton 10.68	76	6	12
Birmingham City 07.76	33	2	1

JONES Philip A.
Liverpool	1 December 1969		
Everton 06.88	0	1	0
Blackpool (L) 03.90	6	0	0
Wigan Athletic 01.91	84	2	2
Bury (NC) 08.93	4	0	0

JONES Thomas E.
Liverpool	11 April 1930		
Everton 01.48	383	0	14

JONES Thomas G.
Connahs Quay	12 October 1917		
Wrexham 11.34	6	0	0
Everton 03.36	165	0	4

JULIUSSEN Albert L.
Blyth	20 February 1920		
Portsmouth 03.48	7	0	4
Everton 09.48	10	0	1

KANCHELSKIS Andrei
Ukraine	23 January 1969		
Manchester United 03.91	96	27	28
Everton 08.95	52	0	21

KAVANAGH Peter J.
Ilford	3 November 1938		
Everton 02.61	6	0	0

KAY Anthony H.
Sheffield	13 May 1937		
Sheffield Wed. 05.54	179	0	10
Everton 12.62	50	0	4

KEARTON Jason B.
Ipswich,Australia	9 July 1969		
Everton 10.88	3	3	0
Stoke City (L) 08.91	16	0	0
Blackpool (L) 01.92	14	0	0
Notts County (L) 01.95	10	0	0
Crewe Alexandra 10.96	145	0	0

KEELEY Glenn M.
Barking	1 September 1954		
Ipswich Town 08.72	4	0	0
Newcastle United 07.74	43	1	2
Blackburn Rovers 08.76	365	523	
Everton (L) 10.82	1	0	0
Oldham Athletic 08.87	10	1	0
Colchester Utd. (L) 02.88	4	0	0
Bolton Wanderers 09.88	20	0	0

KEELEY John J.
Liverpool	18 October 1936		
Everton 05.54	4	0	1

KENDALL Howard
Ryton-on-Tyne	22 May 1946		
PNE 05.63	104	0	13
Everton 03.67	227	2	21
Birmingham City 02.74	115	0	16
Stoke City 08.77	82	0	9
Blackburn Rovers 07.79	79	0	6
Everton (NC) 08.81	4	0	0

KENNY William A.
Liverpool	23 October 1951		
Everton 07.69	10	2	0
Tranmere Rovers 03.75	36	18	6

KENNY William A.
Liverpool	19 September 1973		
Everton 06.92	16	1	1
Oldham Athletic 08.94	4	0	0

KENYON Roger N.
Blackpool	4 January 1949		
Everton 09.66	254	13	6
Bristol City 10.79	4	0	0

KEOWN Martin R.
Oxford	24 July 1966		
Arsenal 02.84	22	0	0
Aston Villa 06.86	109	3	3
Everton 08.89	92	4	0
Arsenal 02.93	208	18	4

KIDD Brian
Manchester	29 May 1949		
Manchester United 06.66	195	8	52
Arsenal 08.74	77	0	30
Manchester City 07.76	97	1	44
Everton 03.79	40	0	12
Bolton Wanderers 05.80	40	3	14

110

KING Andrew E.

Luton	14 August 1956		
Luton Town 07.74	30	3	9
Everton 04.76	150	1	38
QPR 09.80	28	2	9
WBA 09.81	21	4	4
Everton 07.82	43	1	11
Wolverhampton W. 01.85	28	0	10
Luton Town 12.85	3	0	0
Aldershot 08.86	36	0	11

KING John A.

Marylebone	15 April 1938		
Everton 03.56	48	0	1
Bournemouth 07.60	21	0	1
Tranmere Rovers 02.61	239	2	4
Port Vale 07.68	99	2	0

KIRBY George

Liverpool	20 December 1933		
Everton 06.52	26	0	9
Sheffield Wed. 03.59	3	0	0
Plymouth Argyle 01.60	93	0	38
Southampton 09.62	63	0	28
Coventry City 03.64	18	0	10
Swansea City 10.64	26	0	8
Walsall 05.65 74	125		
Brentford 10.68	5	0	1

LABONE Brian L.

Liverpool	23 January 1940		
Everton 07.57	451	0	2

LANGLEY Kevin J.

St Helens	24 May 1964		
Wigan Athletic 05.82	156	4	6
Everton 07.86	16	0	2
Manchester City 03.87	9	0	0
Chester City (L) 01.88	9	0	0
Birmingham City 03.88	74	2	2
Wigan Athletic 09.90	151	6	6

LATCHFORD Robert D.

Birmingham	18 January 1951		
Birmingham City 08.68	158	268	
Everton 02.74	235	1 106	
Swansea City 07.81	87	035	
Coventry City 07.84	11	1	2
Lincoln City 08.85	14	1	2
Newport County 01.86	20	0	5

LAVERICK Robert

Castle Eden	11 June 1938		
Chelsea 06.55	7	0	0
Everton 02.59	22	0	6

Brighton & HA 06.60	63	0	20
Coventry City 07.62	4	0	0

LAWSON David

Wallsend	22 December 1947		
Bradford PA 10.67	13	0	0
Huddersfield Town 05.69	51	0	0
Everton 06.72	124	0	0
Luton Town 10.78	5	0	0
Stockport County 03.79	106	0	0

LEEDER Frederick

Seaton Delaval	15 September 1936		
Everton 03.55	1	0	0
Darlington 07.58	21	0	0
Southport 07.60	63	0	0

LELLO Cyril F.

Ludlow	24 February 1920		
Everton 09.47	237	0	9
Rochdale 11.56	11	0	0

LEWIS Gwynfor

Bangor	22 April 1931		
Everton 05.48	10	0	6
Rochdale 06.56	27	0	11
Chesterfield 02.57	123	0	58

LEYLAND Harry K.

Liverpool	12 May 1930		
Everton 08.50	36	0	0
Blackburn Rovers 08.56	166	0	0
Tranmere Rovers 03.61	180	0	0

LILL Michael J.

Barking	3 August 1936		
Wolverhampton W. 06.54	30	0	15
Everton 02.60	31	0	11
Plymouth Argyle 06.62	21	0	7
Portsmouth 03.63	39	0	5

LIMPAR Anders E.

Sweden	24 August 1965		
Arsenal 07.90	76	20	17
Everton 03.94	51	15	5
Birmingham City 01.97	3	1	0

LINDSAY John S.

Auchinleck	8 August 1924		
Everton 03.51	105	0	2
Bury 05.56	7	0	0

LINEKER Gary W.

Leicester	30 November 1960		
Leicester City 11.78	187	7	95
Everton 07.85	41	0	30
Tottenham H. 07.89	105	0	67

LIVINGSTONE Archibald

Pencaitland	15 November 1915		
Newcastle United 05.35	33	0	5
Bury 06.38	23	0	8
Everton 05.46	4	0	2
Southport 06.47	23	0	2

LLEWELLYN Herbert A.

Golborne	5 February 1939		
Everton 05.56	11	0	2
Crewe Alexandra 07.58	96	0	51
Port Vale 11.60	88	042	
Northampton T. 02.63	1	0	0
Walsall 02.64	17	0	6

LODGE Paul

Liverpool	13 February 1961		
Everton 02.79	20	4	0
Wigan Athletic (L) 08.82	5	0	1
Rotherham Utd (L) 01.83	4	0	0
PNE 02.83	36	2	0
Bolton Wanderers 07.84	4	0	0
Port Vale (L) 11.84	3	0	0
Stockport County 03.85	10	3	2

LYONS Michael

Liverpool	8 December 1951		
Everton 07.69	364	26	48
Sheffield Wed 08.82	129	0	12
Grimsby Town 11.85	50	0	4

McBRIDE Joseph

Glasgow	17 August 1960		
Everton 08.78	51	6	9
Rotherham United 08.82	45	0	12
Oldham Athletic 09.83	28	8	5

McCALL Stuart M.

Leeds	10 June 1964		
Bradford City 06.82	235	33	7
Everton 06.88	99	4	6
Bradford City 06.98	76	1	4

McCANN Gavin P.

Blackpool	10 January 1978		
Everton 07.95	5	6	0
Sunderland 11.98	5	6	0

McCORMICK Harry

Coleraine(NI)	10 January 1924		
Derby County 10.46	7	0	0
Everton 07.48	4	0	0

McDONAGH James M.

Rotherham	6 October 1952		
Rotherham United 10.70	121	0	0
Bolton Wanderers 08.76	161	0	0
Everton 07.80	40	0	0
Bolton Wanderers 08.81	81	0	1
Notts County 07.83	35	0	0
Birmingham C.(L) 09.84	1	0	0
Gillingham (L) 03.85	10	0	0
Sunderland (L) 08.85	7	0	0
Scarborough 11.87	9	0	0
Huddersfield T. 01.88	6	0	0

McDONALD Neil R.

Wallsend	2 November 1965		
Newcastle United 02.83	163	17	24
Everton 08.88	76	14	4
Oldham Athletic 10.91	19	5	1
Bolton Wanderers 07.94	4	0	0
PNE 11.95	20	13	0

McILHATTON John

Ardrossan	3 January 1921		
Everton 04.46	55	0	1

McINTOSH James M.

Dumfries	5 April 1918		
Blackpool 09.35	5	0	0
PNE 11.37	27	0	3
Blackpool 05.46	69	0	25
Everton 03.49	58	0	19

McKENZIE Duncan

Grimsby	10 June 1950		
Nottingham Fores 07.68	105	6	41
Mansfield T. (L) 03.70	7	3	3
Mansfield T. (L) 02.73	6	0	7
Leeds United 08.74	64	2	27
Everton 12.76	48	0	14
Chelsea 09.78	15	0	4
Blackburn Rovers 03.79	74	0	16

McLAUGHLIN John I.

Stirling	3 January 1948		
Everton 10.71	59	2	1

McMAHON Stephen

Liverpool	20 August 1961		
Everton 08.79	99	1	11
Aston Villa 05.83	74	1	7

A Concise Post-War History of Everton

Liverpool 09.85	202	2	29
Manchester City 12.91	83	4	1
Swindon Town 12.94	38	4	0

McNAMARA Anthony

Liverpool	3 October 1929		
Everton 05.50	111	0	22
Liverpool 12.57	10	0	3
Crewe Alexandra 07.58	9	0	2
Bury 09.58	14	0	0

McNAUGHT Kenneth

Kirkcaldy	11 January 1955		
Everton 05.72	64	2	3
Aston Villa 08.77	207	0	8
WBA 08.83	42	0	1
Manchester City(L) 12.84	7	0	0
Sheffield United 07.85	34	0	5

MADAR Mickael R.

Paris,France	8 May 1968		
Everton 12.97	17	2	5

MAHER Aidan

Liverpool	1 December 1946		
Everton 12.64	1	0	0
Plymouth Argyle 10.68	64	0	3
Tranmere Rovers 06.71	2	5	1

MARSHALL Clifford

Liverpool	4 November 1955		
Everton 11.73	6	1	0
Southport 09.76	11	2	0

MARSHALL Ian P.

Oxford	20 March 1966		
Everton 03.84	9	6	0
Oldham Athletic 03.88	165	5	36
Ipswich Town 08.93	79	5	32
Leicester City 08.96	49	34	18

MATERAZZI Marco

Perugia,Italy	19 August 1973		
Everton 07.98	26	1	1

MAYERS Derek

Liverpool	24 January 1935		
Everton 08.52	18	0	7
PNE 05.57	118	0	25
Leeds United 06.61	20	0	5
Bury 07.62	32	0	6
Wrexham 10.63	21	0	2

MEAGAN Michael K.

Dublin	29 May 1934		
Everton 09.52	165	0	1
Huddersfield Town 07.64	118	1	1
Halifax Town 07.68	23	0	0

MEGSON Gary J.

Manchester	2 May 1959		
Plymouth Argyle 05.77	78	0	10
Everton 12.79	20	2	2
Sheffield Wed. 08.81	123	0	13
Newcastle United 11.84	21	3	1
Sheffield Wed. 12.85	107	3	12
Manchester City 01.89	78	4	2
Norwich City 08.92	42	4	1
Lincoln City(NC) 08.95	2	0	0
Shrewsbury T.(NC)09.95	2	0	0

MERCER Joseph

Ellesmere Port	9 August 1914		
Everton 09.32	170	0	1
Arsenal 12.46	247	0	2

MILLIGAN Jamie

Blackpool	3 January 1980		
Everton 06.97	0	3	0

MILLIGAN Michael J.

Manchester	20 February 1967		
Oldham Athletic 02.85	161	1	17
Everton 08.90	16	1	1
Oldham Athletic 07.91	117	0	6
Norwich City 06.94	113	11	5

MIMMS Robert A.

York	12 October 1963		
Rotherham United 11.81	83	0	0
Everton 06.85	29	0	0
Notts County (L) 03.86	2	0	0
Sunderland (L) 12.86	4	0	0
Blackburn Rov.(L) 01.87	6	0	0
Manchester City(L) 09.87	3	0	0
Tottenham H. 02.88	37	0	0
Blackburn Rovers 12.90	126	2	0
Crystal Palace(NC) 08.96	1	0	0
PNE09.96	27	0	0
Rotherham United 08.97	43	0	0
York City 08.98	63	0	0
Mansfield Town 03.00	5	0	0

MOORE Eric

St Helens	16 July 1926		
Everton 02.49	171	0	0
Chesterfield 01.57	6	0	0
Tranmere Rovers 07.57	36	0	0

113

MOORE Joe-Max

United States	23 February 1971			
Everton 11.99	11	4		6

MORRISSEY John J.

Liverpool	18 April 1940			
Liverpool 05.57	36	0		6
Everton 09.62	257	2		43
Oldham Athletic 05.72	6	0		1

MORRISSEY John J.

Liverpool	8 March 1965			
Everton 03.83	1	0		0
Wolverhampton W. 08.85	5	5		1
Tranmere Rovers 10.85	396	74		50

MOUNTFIELD Derek N.

Liverpool	2 November 1962			
Tranmere Rovers 11.80	26	0		1
Everton 06.82	100	6		19
Aston Villa 06.88	88	2		9
Wolverhampton W. 11.91	79	4		4
Carlisle United 08.94	30	1		3
Northampton T. 10.95	4	0		0
Walsall 11.95	8	0		0
Scarborough 01.99	5	1		0

MYHRE Thomas

Sarpsborg,Norway	16 October 1973			
Everton 11.97	64	0		0
Birmingham C. (L) 03.00	7	0		0

NEVIN Patrick K.F.M.

Glasgow	6 September 1963			
Chelsea 07.83	190	3		36
Everton 07.88	81	28		16
Tranmere Rov. (L) 03.92	8	0		0
Tranmere Rovers 08.92	181	12		30

NEWELL Michael C.

Liverpool	27 January 1965			
Crewe Alexandra 09.83	3	0		0
Wigan Athletic 10.83	64	8		25
Luton Town 01.86	62	1		18
Leicester City 09.87	81	0		21
Everton 07.89	48	20		15
Blackburn Rovers 11.91	113	17		28
Birmingham City 07.96	11	4		1
West Ham Utd(L) 12.96	6	1		0
Bradford City(L) 03.97	7	0		0
Crewe Alexandra 03.99	1	3		0
Blackpool 01.00	12	1		2

NEWTON Henry A.

Nottingham	18 February 1944			
Nottingham Forest 06.61	282	0		17
Everton 10.70	76	1		5
Derby County 09.73	111	6		5
Walsall 07.77	16	0		0

NEWTON Keith R.

Manchester	23 June 1941			
Blackburn Rovers 10.58	306	0		9
Everton 12.69	48	1		1
Burnley 06.72	209	0		5

O'CONNOR Jonathan

Darlington	29 October 1976			
Everton 10.93	3	2		0
Sheffield United 02.98	2	2		0

O'HARA Edward A.

Glasgow	28 October 1935			
Everton 06.58	29	0		2
Rotherham United 02.60	20	0		3
Barnsley 07.62	127	0		36

O'KANE John A.

Nottingham	15 November 1974			
Manchester United 01.93	1	1		0
Bury (L) 10.96	2	2		2
Bury (L) 01.97	9	0		1
Bradford City (L) 10.97	7	0		0
Everton 01.98	14	0		0
Burnley (L) 10.98	8	0		0
Bolton Wanderers 10.99	7	4		1

O'KEEFE Eamonn G.

Manchester	13 October 1953			
Everton 07.79	26	14		6
Wigan Athletic 01.82	56	2		25
Port Vale 07.83	50	9		17
Blackpool 03.85	33	3		23
Chester City 03.89	12	5		4

OLDROYD Darren R.

Ormskirk	1 November 1966			
Everton 11.84	0	1		0
Wolverhampton W. 08.86	10	0		0

O'NEILL James A.

Dublin	13 October 1931			
Everton 05.49	201	0		0
Stoke City 07.60	130	0		0
Darlington 03.64	32	0		0
Port Vale 02.65	42	0		0

A Concise Post-War History of Everton

OSTER John M.

Boston	8 December 1978		
Grimsby Town 07.96	21	3	3
Everton 07.97	22	18	1

OWEN Terence L.

Liverpool	11 September 1949		
Everton 12.66	2	0	0
Bradford City 06.70	41	11	6
Chester City 06.72	161	15	41
Cambridge United 08.77	1	0	0
Rochdale 09.77	80	3	21
Port Vale 07.79	14	4	3

PARKER Alexander H.

Irvine	2 August 1935		
Everton 06.58	198	0	5
Southport 09.65	76	0	0

PARKINSON Joseph S.

Eccles	11 June 1971		
Wigan Athletic 03.89	115	4	6
Bournemouth 07.93	30	0	1
Everton 03.94	88	2	3

PARNELL Roy

Birkenhead	8 October 1943		
Everton 10.60	3	0	0
Tranmere Rovers 08.64	105	0	2
Bury 02.67	97	0	2

PAYNE James B.

Liverpool	10 March 1926		
Liverpool 11.44	224	0	37
Everton 04.56	5	0	2

PEARSON James F.

Falkirk	24 March 1953		
Everton 07.74	76	17	15
Newcastle United 08.78	11	0	3

PEJIC Michael

Chesterton	25 January 1950		
Stoke City 01.68	274	0	6
Everton 02.77	76	0	2
Aston Villa 09.79	10	0	0

PEMBRIDGE Mark A.

Merthyr Tydfil	29 November 1970		
Luton Town 07.89	60	0	6
Derby County 06.92	108	2	28
Sheffield Wed. 07.95	88	5	12
Everton 07.99	29	2	2

PHELAN Terence M.

Manchester	16 March 1967		
Leeds United 08.84	12	2	0
Swansea City 07.86	45	0	0
Wimbledon 07.87	155	4	1
Manchester City 08.92	102	1	2
Chelsea 11.95	13	2	0
Everton 01.97	23	2	0
Crystal Palace (L) 10.99	14	0	0
Fulham 02.00	17	0	2

PICKERING Frederick

Blackburn	19 January 1941		
Blackburn Rovers 01.58	123	0	59
Everton 03.64	97	0	56
Birmingham City 08.67	74	0	27
Blackpool 06.69	48	1	24
Blackburn Rovers 03.71	11	0	2

POINTON Neil G.

Church Warsop	28 November 1964		
Scunthorpe United 08.82	159	0	2
Everton 11.85	95	7	5
Manchester City 07.90	74	0	2
Oldham Athletic 09.92	92	3	3

POTTS Harry

Hetton-le-Hole	22 October 1920		
Burnley 11.37	165	0	47
Everton 10.50	59	0	15

POWELL Aubrey

Swansea	19 April 1918		
Leeds United 11.35	112	0	25
Everton 07.48	35	0	5
Birmingham City 08.50	15	0	1

POWER Paul C.

Manchester	30 October 1953		
Manchester City 09.73	358	7	26
Everton 06.86	52	2	6

RADOSAVLJEVIC Predrag(Preki)

Yugoslavia	24 June 1963		
Everton 08.92	22	24	4
Portsmouth 07.94	30	10	5

RANKIN Andrew G.

Bootle	11 May 1944		
Everton 10.61	85	0	0
Watford 11.71	299	0	0
Huddersfield T. 12.79	71	0	0

RANKIN George

Liverpool	29 January 1930		
Everton 08.48	36	0	0
Southport 07.56	144	0	0

RATCLIFFE Kevin

Deeside	12 November 1960		
Everton 11.78	356	3	2
Cardiff City (NC) 01.93	25	0	1
Derby County (NC) 1.94	6	0	0
Chester City 07.94	23	0	0

REA Kenneth W.

Liverpool	17 February 1935		
Everton 06.52	46	0	0

REES Barrie G.

Rhyl	4 February 1944		
Everton 09.61	4	0	2
Brighton & HA 01.65	12	0	1

REHN Stefan J.

Sweden	22 September 1966		
Everton 06.89	1	3	0

REID Peter

Huyton	20 June 1956		
Bolton Wanderers 05.74	222	3	23
Everton 12.82	155	4	8
QPR 02.89	29	0	1
Manchester City 12.89	90	13	1
Southampton(NC) 09.93	7	0	0
Notts Co. (NC) 02.94	5	0	0
Bury (NC) 07.94	1	0	0

RICHARDSON Kevin

Newcastle	4 December 1962		
Everton 12.80	95	14	16
Watford 09.86	39	0	2
Arsenal 08.87	88	8	5
Aston Villa 08.91	142	1	13
Coventry City 02.95	75	3	0
Southampton 09.97	25	3	0
Barnsley 07.98	24	2	0

RIDEOUT Paul D.

Bournemouth	14 August 1964		
Swindon Town 08.81	90	5	38
Aston Villa 06.83	50	4	19
Southampton 07.88	68	7	19
Swindon Town (L) 03.91	9	0	1
Notts County 09.91	9	2	3
Everton 08.92	86	26	29

RIMMER Neill

Liverpool	13 November 1967		
Everton 04.84	0	1	0
Ipswich Town 08.85	19	3	3
Wigan Athletic 07.88	184	6	10

RIMMER Stuart A.

Southport	12 October 1964		
Everton 10.82	3	0	0
Chester City 01.85	110	4	67
Watford 03.88	10	0	1
Notts County 11.88	3	1	2
Walsall 02.89	85	3	31
Barnsley 03.91	10	5	1
Chester City 08.91	213	34	67
Rochdale (L) 09.94	3	0	0
PNE (L) 12.94	0	2	0

RING Thomas

Glasgow	8 August 1930		
Everton 01.60	27	0	6
Barnsley 11.61	21	0	1

RIOCH Bruce D.

Aldershot	6 September 1947		
Luton Town 09.64	148	1	46
Aston Villa 07.69	149	5	34
Derby County 02.74	106	0	34
Everton 12.76	30	0	3
Derby County 11.77	40	1	4
Birmingham C. (L) 12.78	3	0	0
Sheffield United(L) 03.79	8	0	1
Torquay United 10.80	64	7	6

ROBINSON Neil

Liverpool	20 April 1957		
Everton 05.74	13	3	1
Swansea City 10.79	114	9	7
Grimsby Town 09.84	109	0	6
Darlington 07.88	36	2	1

ROSS Trevor W.

Ashton-under-Lyne	16 January 1957		
Arsenal 06.74	57	1	5
Everton 11.77	120	6	16
Portsmouth (L) 10.82	5	0	0
Sheffield Utd.(L) 12.82	4	0	0
Sheffield United 01.84	4	0	0
Bury 08.84	96	2	11

ROWETT Gary

Bromsgrove	6 March 1974		
Cambridge United 08.91	51	12	9
Everton 05.94	2	2	0
Blackpool (L) 01.95	17	0	0

Derby County 07.95	101	4	3
Birmingham City 08.98	87	0	6

ROYLE Joseph

Liverpool	8 April 1949		
Everton 06.66	229	3	102
Manchester City 12.74	98	1	23
Bristol City 11.77	100	1	18
Norwich City 08.80	40	2	9

SAGAR Edward

Campsall	7 February 1910		
Everton 03.29	463	0	0

SAMWAYS Vincent

Bethnal Green	27 October 1968		
Tottenham Hotspur10.85	165	28	11
Everton 08.94	17	6	2
Wol'ampton W.(L)12.95	3	0	0
Birmingham C.(L) 02.96	12	0	0

SANDERS Alan

Salford	31 January 1934		
Everton 07.56	56	0	0
Swansea City 11.59	92	0	0
Brighton & HA 01.63	80	0	0

SANSOM Kenneth G.

Camberwell	26 September 1958		
Crystal Palace 12.75	172	0	3
Arsenal 08.80	314	0	6
Newcastle United 12.88	20	0	0
QPR 06.89	64	0	0
Coventry City 03.91	51	0	0
Everton 02.93	6	1	1
Brentford 03.93	8	0	0
Watford (NC) 08.94	1	0	0

SAUNDERS George E.

Birkenhead	1 March 1918		
Everton 02.39	133	0	0

SAUNDERS Ronald

Birkenhead	6 November 1932		
Everton 02.51	3	0	0
Gillingham 05.57	49	0	20
Portsmouth 09.58	236	0	145
Watford 09.64	39	0	18
Charlton Athletic 08.65	64	1	24

SCOTT Alexander S.

Falkirk	22 November 1936		
Everton 02.63	149	0	23

SCOTT Peter W.

Liverpool	19 September 1952		
Everton 07.70	42	2	1
Southport (L) 01.74	4	0	0
York City 12.75	99	1	3
Aldershot 03.79	114	7	2

SEARGENT Steven C.

Liverpool	2 January 1951		
Everton 07.68	77	3	1

SHARP Graeme M.

Glasgow	16 October 1960		
Everton 04.80	306	16	111
Oldham Athletic 07.91	103	4	30

SHARPLES George F.V.

Ellesmere Port	20 September 1943		
Everton 09.60	10	0	0
Blackburn Rovers 03.65	99	4	5
Southport 07.71	23	2	0

SHAW Stuart

Liverpool	9 October 1944		
Everton 12.61	3	0	0
Crystal Palace 12.66			
Southport 03.67	66	1	6
Port Vale 07.69	1	2	0

SHEEDY Kevin M.

Builth Wells	21 October 1959		
Hereford United 10.76	47	4	4
Liverpool 07.78	1	2	0
Everton 08.82	263	11	67
Newcastle United 03.92	36	1	4
Blackpool 07.93	25	1	1

SHORT Craig J.

Bridlington	25 June 1968		
Scarborough 10.87	61	2	7
Notts County 07.89	128	0	6
Derby County 09.92	118	0	9
Everton 07.95	90	9	4
Blackburn Rovers 07.99	17	0	0

SIMONSEN Steven P.

South Shields	3 April 1979		
Tranmere Rovers 10.96	35	0	0
Everton 09.98	0	1	0

SMALLMAN David P.

Connahs Quay	22 March 1953		
Wrexham 11.71	100	1	38
Everton 03.75	19	2	6

117

SMITH Derek L.

Liverpool	5 July 1946		
Everton 11.63	3	1	0
Tranmere Rovers 03.68	77	5	21

SMITH John

Liverpool	14 March 1953		
Everton 09.70	2	0	0
Carlisle United 06.76	4	1	0
Southport (L) 02.77	17	1	2

SNODIN Ian

Rotherham	15 August 1963		
Doncaster Rovers 08.80	181	7	25
Leeds United 05.85	51	0	6
Everton 01.87	142	6	3
Sunderland (L) 10.94	6	0	0
Oldham Athletic 01.95	55	2	0
Scarborough 08.97	33	2	0

SOUTHALL Neville

Llandudno	16 September 1958		
Bury 06.80	39	0	0
Everton 07.81	578	0	0
Port Vale (L) 01.83	9	0	0
Southend Utd. (L) 12.97	9	0	0
Stoke City 02.98	12	0	0
Torquay United 12.98	25	0	0
Bradford City 09.99	1	0	0

SPEED Gary A.

Mancot	8 September 1969		
Leeds United 06.88	231	17	39
Everton 07.96	58	0	15
Newcastle United 02.98	83	4	14

SPENCER John

Glasgow	11 September 1970		
Chelsea 08.92	75	28	36
QPR 11.96	47	1	22
Everton 03.98	5	4	0

STANLEY Gary E.

Burton	4 March 1954		
Chelsea 03.71	105	4	15
Everton 08.79	52	0	1
Swansea City 10.81	60	12	4
Portsmouth 01.84	43	4	1
Bristol City 08.88	8	2	0

STEVEN Trevor M.

Berwick	21 September 1963		
Burnley 09.81	74	2	11
Everton 07.83	210	4	48

STEVENS Dennis

Dudley	30 November 1933		
Bolton Wanderers 12.50	273	0	90
Everton 03.62	120	0	20
Oldham Athletic 12.65	33	0	0
Tranmere Rovers 03.67	28	4	3

STEVENS Gary M.

Barrow	27 March 1963		
Everton 03.81	207	1	8
Tranmere Rovers 09.94	126	1	2

STEVENSON Alexander E.

Dublin	9 August 1912		
Everton 01.34	255	0	82

STUART Graham C.

Tooting	24 October 1970		
Chelsea 06.89	70	17	14
Everton 08.93	116	20	23
Sheffield United 11.97	52	1	11
Charlton Athletic 03.99	42	4	11

STYLES Arthur

Liverpool	3 September 1949		
Everton 08.67	22	1	0
Birmingham City 02.74	71	3	4
Peterborough Utd. 07.78	32	0	1
Portsmouth 07.79	28	0	0

SUTHERLAND John F.

Cork	10 February 1932		
Everton 05.50	6	0	0
Chesterfield 06.57	47	0	0
Crewe Alexandra 11.58	47	0	1

TANSEY James

Liverpool	29 January 1929		
Everton 05.48	133	0	0
Crewe Alexandra 06.60	9	0	0

TELFER George A.

Liverpool	6 July 1955		
Everton 08.72	81	18	20
Scunthorpe United 12.81	34	2	11
PNE (NC) 08.83	0	2	0

A Concise Post-War History of Everton

TEMPLE Derek W.
Liverpool	13 November 1938		
Everton 08.56	231	1	72
PNE 09.67	75	1	14

THOMAS David
Kirkby-in-Ashfield	5 October 1950		
Burnley 10.67	153	4	19
QPR 10.72	181	1	28
Everton 08.77	71	0	4
Wolverhampton W. 10.79	10	0	0
Middlesbrough 03.82	13	0	1
Portsmouth 07.82	24	6	0

THOMAS Edward
Newton-le-Willows	23 October 1933		
Everton 10.51	86	0	39
Blackburn Rovers 02.60	37	0	9
Swansea City 07.62	68	0	21
Derby County 08.64	102	3	43
Leyton Orient 09.67	11	0	2

THOMAS Michael R.
Caersws	7 July 1954		
Wrexham 05.72	217	13	33
Manchester Utd. 11.78	90	0	11
Everton 08.81	10	0	0
Brighton & HA 11.81	18	2	0
Stoke City 08.82	57	0	14
Chelsea 01.84	43	1	9
WBA 09.85	20	0	0
Derby County (L) 03.86	9	0	0
Shrewsbury Town 08.88	40	0	1
Leeds United 06.89	3	0	0
Stoke City (L) 03.90	8	0	0
Stoke City 08.90	32	6	7
Wrexham 07.91	34	0	2

THOMAS Anthony
Liverpool	12 July 1971		
Tranmere Rovers 02.89	254	3	12
Everton 8.97	6	2	0

THOMSEN Claus
Denmark	31 May 1970		
Ipswich Town 06.94	77	4	7
Everton 01.97	17	7	1

THOMSON George M.
Edinburgh	19 October 1936		
Everton 11.60	73	0	1
Brentford 11.63	160	2	5

TILER Carl
Sheffield	11 February 1970		
Barnsley 08.88	67	4	3
Nottingham Forest 05.91	67	2	1
Swindon Town (L) 11.94	2	0	0
Aston Villa 10.95	10	2	1
Sheffield United 03.97	23	2	0
Everton 11.97	21	0	1
Charlton Athletic 09.98	27	0	1

TODD Colin
Chester-le-Street	12 December 1948		
Sunderland 12.66	170	3	3
Derby County 02.71	293	0	6
Everton 09.78	32	0	1
Birmingham City 09.79	92	1	0
Nottingham Forest 08.82	36	0	0
Oxford United 02.84	12	0	0
Luton Town 10.84	20	0	0

TOMLINSON John
Bebington	26 June 1934		
Everton 06.52	2	0	0
Chesterfield 06.57	47	0	5

TREBILCOCK Michael
Callington	29 November 1944		
Plymouth Argyle 12.62	71	0	27
Everton 12.65	11	0	3
Portsmouth 01.68	99	10	33
Torquay United 07.72	23	1	10

TURNER David
Derby	26 December 1948		
Everton 10.66	1	0	0
Southport 05.70	69	2	0

TYRER Alan
Liverpool	8 December 1942		
Everton 12.59	9	0	2
Mansfield Town 07.63	41	0	5
Bury 08.67	20	0	0
Workington 07.68	228	15	18

UNSWORTH David G.
Chorley	16 October 1973		
Everton 06.92	108	8	11
West Ham United 08.97	32	0	2
Aston Villa 07.98	0	0	0
Everton 08.98	65	2	7

VAN DEN HAUWE Patrick W.R.
Belgium	16 December 1960		
Birmingham City 08.78	119	4	1
Everton 09.84	134	1	2

Tottenham Hotspur 08.89	110	6	0
Millwall 09.93	27	0	0

VARAIDI Imre

Paddington	8 July 1959		
Sheffield United 04.78	6	4	4
Everton 03.79	22	4	6
Newcastle United 08.81	81	0	39
Sheffield Wed. 08.83	72	4	33
WBA 07.85	30	2	9
Manchester City 10.86	56	9	26
Sheffield Wed. 09.88	14	8	3
Leeds United 02.90	21	5	5
Luton Town (L) 03.92	5	1	1
Oxford United (L) 01.92	3	2	0
Rotherham United03.92	55	12	25
Mansfield T. (NC)08.95	1	0	0
Scunthorpe U.(NC) 09.95	0	2	0

VEALL Raymond J.

Skegness	16 March 1943		
Doncaster Rovers 03.61	19	0	6
Everton 09.61	11	0	1
PNE 05.65	11	0	0
Huddersfield T. 12.65	12	0	1

VERNON Royston T.

Prestatyn	14 April 1937		
Blackburn Rovers 03.55	131	0	49
Everton 02.60	176	0	101
Stoke City 03.65	84	3	22
Halifax Town 01.70	4	0	0

WAINWRIGHT Edward F.

Southport	22 June 1924		
Everton 03.44	207	0	68
Rochdale 06.56	100	0	27

WAKENSHAW Robert A.

Ponteland	22 December 1965		
Everton 12.83	2	1	1
Carlisle United 09.85	6	2	2
Doncaster Rov.(L) 03.86	8	0	3
Rochdale 09.86	28	1	5
Crewe Alexandra 06.87	18	4	1

WALSH Derek

Hamilton	24 October 1967		
Everton 10.84	1	0	0
Carlisle United 08.88	108	13	6

WALSH Michael A.

Chorley	13 August 1954		
Blackpool 11.71	172	8	72
Everton 08.78	18	3	1

QPR 03.79	13	5	3

WALSH Michael T.

Manchester	20 June 1956		
Bolton Wanderers 07.74	169	8	4
Everton 08.81	20	0	0
Norwich City (L) 10.82	5	0	0
Burnley (L) 12.82	3	0	0
Manchester City 10.83	3	1	0
Blackpool 02.84	146	7	5

WARD Mark W.

Huyton	10 October 1962		
Oldham Athletic 07.83	84	0	12
West Ham United 08.85	163	2	12
Manchester City 12.89	55	0	14
Everton 08.91	82	1	6
Birmingham City 03.94	63	0	7
Huddersfield T. 03.96	7	1	0
Wigan Ath. (NC) 09.96	5	0	0

WARD Mitchum D.

Sheffield	19 June 1971		
Sheffield United 07.89	135	19	11
Crewe Alex. (L) 11.90	4	0	1
Everton 11.97	18	6	0

WARZYCHA Robert

Poland	20 June 1963		
Everton 03.91	51	21	6

WATSON David

Liverpool	20 November 1961		
Norwich City 11.80	212	0	11
Everton 08.86	419	4	23

WATSON Gordon T.

Wolsingham	1 March 1914		
Everton 01.33	61	0	1

WEBBER Keith J.

Cardiff	5 January 1943		
Everton 02.60	4	0	0
Brighton & HA 04.63	35	0	14
Wrexham09.64	73	0	33
Doncaster Rov. 07.66	63	4	18
Chester City 06.69	66	8	14
Stockport County 07.71	36	4	7

WEIR David G.

Falkirk	10 May 1970		
Everton 02.99	44	3	2

WEST Gordon

Darfield	24 April 1943		
Blackpool 05.61	31	0	0
Everton 03.62	335	0	0
Tranmere Rovers 10.75	17	0	0

WHITESIDE Norman

Belfast	7 May 1965		
Manchester United 07.82	193	13	47
Everton 07.89	27	2	9

WHITTLE Alan

Liverpool	10 March 1950		
Everton 07.65	72	2	21
Crystal Palace 12.72	103	5	19
Leyton Orient 09.76	47	3	6
Bournemouth(NC) 01.81	8	1	0

WIGNALL Frank

Chorley	21 August 1939		
Everton 05.58	33	0	15
Nottingham Forest 06.63	156	1	47
Wolverhampton W. 03.68	32	0	15
Derby County 02.69	29	16	15
Mansfield Town 11.71	50	6	15

WILKINSON Paul

Louth	30 October 1964		
Grimsby Town 10.82	69	2	27
Everton 03.85	19	12	7
Nottingham Forest 03.87	32	2	5
Watford 08.88	133	1	52
Middlesbrough 08.91	161	5	49
Oldham Ath. (L)10.95	4	0	1
Watford (L) 12.95	4	0	0
Luton Town (L) 03.96	3	0	0
Barnsley 07.96	48	1	9
Millwall 09.97	22	8	3
Northampton T. 07.98	12	3	1

WILLIAMS Graham G.

Wrexham	31 December 1936		
Bradford City 08.55	8	0	2
Everton 03.56	31	0	6
Swansea City 02.59	89	0	20
Wrexham 07.64	24	0	6
Tranmere Rovers 08.66	73	1	12
Port Vale 07.68	21	2	1

WILLIAMSON Daniel A.

West Ham	5 December 1973		
West Ham United 07.92	47	4	5
Doncaster Rov. (L) 10.93	10	3	1
Everton 08.97	15	0	0

WILSON Alan

Liverpool	17 November 1952		
Everton 07.70	2	0	0
Southport 07.75	134	0	13
Torquay United 06.78	38	4	2

WILSON Ian W.

Aberdeen	27 March 1958		
Leicester City 04.79	276	9	17
Everton 09.87	24	10	1
Derby Co. (NC) 02.91	11	0	0
Bury 08.91	21	3	1
Wigan Ath. (NC)08.92	5	0	0

WILSON Ramon (Ray)

Shirebrook	17 December 1934		
Huddersfield T. 08.52	266	0	6
Everton 07.64	114	2	0
Oldham Athletic 07.69	25	0	0
Bradford City 07.70	2	0	0

WOOD George

Douglas	26 September 1952		
Blackpool 01.72	117	0	0
Everton 08.77	103	0	0
Arsenal 08.80	60	0	0
Crystal Palace 08.83	192	0	0
Cardiff City 01.88	67	0	0
Blackpool (L) 03.90	15	0	0
Hereford United 08.90	41	0	0

WOODS Maurice (Matt)

Skelmersdale	1 November 1931		
Everton 11.49	8	0	1
Blackburn Rovers 11.56	260	0	2
Luton Town 07.65	34	0	0
Stockport County 07.66	85	0	2

WRIGHT Bernard P.

Birmingham	17 September 1952		
Walsall 09.71	15	0	2
Everton 02.72	10	1	2
Walsall 01.73	145	7	38
Bradford City 02.77	65	1	13
Port Vale 06.78	76	0	23

WRIGHT Mark A.

Manchester	29 January 1970		
Everton 06.88	1	0	0
Blackpool (L) 08.90	3	0	0
Huddersfield T. 03.91	25	7	1
Wigan Athletic 11.93	27	3	1

WRIGHT Thomas J.

Liverpool	21 October 1944		
Everton 03.63	307	1	4

WRIGHT William

Liverpool	28 April 1958		
Everton 01.77	164	2	10
Birmingham City 07.83	111	0	8
Chester City (L) 02.86	6	0	1
Carlisle United 08.86	87	0	3

XAVIER Abel

Mozambique	30 November 1972		
Everton 08.99	18	2	0

YOUDS Edward P.

Liverpool	3 May 1970		
Everton 06.88	5	3	0
Cardiff City (L) 12.89	0	1	0
Wrexham (L) 02.90	20	0	2
Ipswich Town 11.91	38	12	1
Bradford City 01.95	85	0	8
Charlton Athletic 03.98	29	1	2

YOUNG Alexander

Loanhead	3 February 1937		
Everton 11.60	227	1	77
Stockport County 11.68	23	0	5